FUNDAMENTAL$

OF FINANCE

AN INTERACTIVE BOOK

This book is written as a source of information only. The information contained herein should by no means be considered a substitute for the advice, decisions, or judgment of the reader's financial or other professional advisors. Thus, neither the publisher nor the author assumes liability of any kind for any losses that may be sustained as a result of applying the methods suggested in this book. Any such liability has been disclaimed.

Printed in the United States of America

Contents

Acknowledgments	iii
Introduction	v
Chapter 1: Recognizing Your Spending Characteristics	1
Chapter 2: Understanding Financial Institutions	11
Chapter 3: Taking On Debt	29
Chapter 4: Setting Goals and Creating Plans	63
Chapter 5: Looking Toward Retirement	89
Final Words	103
Credit Repair Templates	105
Money Management Tools	115
Notes	128

Acknowledgments

I want to thank God for giving me wisdom and trusting me with the mission. Being given the vision to inspire, guide, and impart wisdom is a welcomed task. I am dedicated to helping those whom I encounter.

I'd like to thank my clients—future and legacy clients—for trusting me with your financial situations. And for understanding the value of my expertise, allowing me to serve and coach you into better lifestyles.

Lastly, I would like to thank my parents for always emphasizing the importance of education. Knowledge is power. I am forever grateful for that foundation.

Introduction

Imagine making your first real adult decision and finding out months later that you owed $768 on a credit card that you never applied for. You'd feel confused and scared, right? Well, that's exactly what happened to me.

When I was nineteen, I opted out of living in an on-campus dorm, instead choosing to rent a two-bedroom apartment with my best friend, who was attending the same college. We had no trouble getting approved for the apartment, but I didn't know that I should've received a copy of my credit report. It wasn't until I was attempting to pay off my only Visa card that I learned what was actually in my report: $768 in collections for a Capital One card that had never been paid.

I reached out to the collection agency to let them know this was an error. They informed me that they had paperwork showing I signed for the card and verified that the card was sent to my home address—my mother's house. They then showed me proof that items had been sent to my family's home and signed for, meaning someone had been using that card. I felt violated. Used. Betrayed. It was then that I understood I'm responsible for anything that's under my Social Security number, whether I initiate it or not.

The company said the only way to remove the debt from my report was to fill out a police report saying that it was fraudulent. But understanding what filling out a police report would do to the family member who had been using my card, I was not willing to press charges. I instead decided to speak to the members of my household, explaining how their actions had negative ramifications for my financial future. I then told everyone that if anything like that ever happened again, I would not hesitate to move forward with pressing charges.

To begin cleaning up my credit, I went to a credit union and asked for a consolidation loan for my Visa card, which had a balance of approximately $4,000, and the Capital One card. I used my car as collateral, meaning if I didn't pay back the loan, then my car would belong to the credit union. Since I was getting rid of all the open accounts on my credit report, the credit union also offered me the option to get a secured credit card with a $300 limit, which would enable me to more quickly reestablish credit.

Have you ever had a stressful money situation? I was just starting my financial career when this incident occurred, and it was embarrassing to have to ask for help. Had it not been for my representative's knowledge and her willingness to explain my options, I would have felt hopeless.

Yet experience is the best teacher. We learn not to repeat unfavorable behavior. So, I finished my degree and worked at the credit union, then branched off into mortgage loan processing and banking. Over the next twenty-plus years, I expanded my industry knowledge, made some mistakes personally, and noticed a need that traditional banks are unable to fill: resources for the average person to learn and understand their finances.

With a drive to help more people, I began a financial consulting business, DG Revenue Management, in 2016. This business offers accounting services, financial coaching, and more, all tailored toward the specific needs of individuals and businesses. Since February 2020, it has also hosted a three-part financial competency seminar for adults and youth ages thirteen to eighteen, covering basic banking, money management, and credit awareness.

Finally, in 2021, I obtained certification as a HUD Housing Counselor while working with a nonprofit as a Financial Capability Coach. I then established the Revenue Management Foundation, a nonprofit dedicated to reducing the wealth distribution gap by providing low-income communities with financial education and resources.

That's ultimately why I wrote this book: to increase access to crucial financial knowledge. In *Fundamentals of Finance*, you will read about some of the financial hardships I dealt with, as well as some of the wins I've had. My aim is to help you avoid the mistakes I made and to recover more quickly from those you've already faced.

Whether you're a teenager looking toward college or a divorcee starting over, this book will teach you money management principles that you can implement immediately, such as goal setting, saving, and retirement planning. You will also learn to recognize your spending characteristics, understand how financial institutions operate, and responsibly take on debt and utilize credit.

This may seem daunting, especially if you feel like you don't have enough money. Remember, no amount is too small to start saving, and a "nuclear family" dynamic is not the only one that can have success in finances.

On the other hand, you may be wondering if this is a book that you need. The answer is…YES! There is no specific dollar amount that makes you invincible against financial strain. I can assure you, there is something here for you.

Consider, does your family talk about finances? If you have a job, do you save some of each paycheck, or do you spend it all immediately? Do you know how credit is calculated and how it can affect your life long-term? These are the kinds of questions we'll address in this book.

The best part is, through the experiences I'll share and the exercises I've compiled, you will learn to think differently about your relationship with money. So, grab your favorite throw blanket and let's get started!

CHAPTER 1
Recognizing Your Spending Characteristics

As an adolescent, I witnessed my mother spending money on what seemed like experiences. She liked to travel frequently to Canada to play bingo and visit the casino, and she always brought home saltwater taffy when she made trips to Atlantic City with friends. At home, she participated in local bowling leagues weekly and attended cabaret parties with bowling friends. It seemed, to me, as if she was enjoying life.

Both of my parents worked, but money was tighter after my father was no longer in the home. In fact, I don't think my mother achieved financial stability until I was sixteen years old, which is odd since she had an associate's degree in accounting. She had book knowledge but no applied money management skills. When she had money, she was open to giving and spending it; when she didn't, we just went without extracurriculars.

My dad was more strategic in how he spent money. He planned, saved, and prepared for the future earlier in my life. But while there were plenty of conversations in my home about how vices can affect your physical health, there were none about how they can affect your financial health.

As a result, I had a very nonchalant attitude toward money. I believed there would always be more.

It's important to consider our family's financial experiences because those experiences impact how we view money as teenagers and adults. For example, people who view money as a scarce commodity tend to hoard it; those who view it as unreliable tend to overspend when they receive lump sums; those who view it as the root of all evil tend to reject opportunities to make more.

In this chapter, we will discuss common spending characteristics so you can gain awareness of how you currently view and use money. That way, you can be more intentional in making financial decisions moving forward.

What Are Spending Characteristics?

As a young adult, I didn't spend much, if only because for years there was never an excess of money to spend. Living paycheck to paycheck doesn't afford you the ability to mess up. That said, I did like to give to those who were close to me, like my mother—just never to the extreme of putting myself in financial trouble.

Fast-forward to today, and God has blessed me with savings in the bank. Still, I often feel buyer's remorse before even leaving a store and end up putting back 90 percent of my cart. I believe that comes from my upbringing, from being told that having unnecessary things is not good. So, while I've had multiple spending characteristics throughout my life, I'm innately a saver.

Often, people adopt different characteristics at different points in their lives. A man looking to raise a family, for instance, may spend years as a security seeker. Women with children are frequently savers because they are planning ahead, while a single person with no children sometimes spends an extended period as a risk taker.

Again, the purpose of identifying your spending characteristics is to understand your habits and determine whether they should change because of your current life status or financial situation. Let's unpack all six of them now.

The Giver

Children tend to be possessive of people and things that they love, such as their mom and their toys. As their brains develop, though, their parents begin to teach them that sharing means caring. This principle, I believe, is where the giver spending characteristic originates.

Parents share food and snacks and, of course, give money to their children. As a result, children begin to automatically associate giving with kindness and care. Think about it: Most children, once they've learned to share and interact with other kids, will give without question and without taking themselves into consideration.

The sense of loss people feel when giving away something valuable tends to begin during adolescence. It's a rite of passage understanding that sometimes you give and get nothing back in return. At a certain point, our brains begin to understand that giving away things you value just because someone asks is not always the right thing to do. Not everyone has this epiphany at the same time, and that is why we encounter adult givers.

Now don't misunderstand; giving is a good thing. But this category, "The Giver," pertains not only to individuals who give to help others when they have extra money but also to those who give even when it means that they go without.

The giver may have a hard time saying "no" because they fear ostracization or because they are conflict avoidant. Whatever the case, their goal should be to learn how to provide support without harming their own financial well-being.

The Spender

Often, a spender is someone who puts too much emphasis on their status. Their self-worth is based on material things, so they cope with everyday stressors by shopping—what they call "retail therapy." But it should be called "avoid-the-problem-and-put-myself-in-more-debt therapy."

Most people, when purchasing items, feel a sense of loss; there's a discomfort in seeing money dwindle from their bank accounts. Spenders, however, feel a boost in dopamine, like they're on a high. Naturally, when we feel happy, we will do anything to keep feeling that way, hence the overspending.

There are a couple of ways a spending characteristic develops. First, a person may come from a home environment where gift giving is highly valued, where money is used as positive reinforcement, and/or where new items are given in lieu of emotional support. Spending, as a result, is normal for them. Second, a person who was a "have not" may either work their way up or get a windfall into a higher tax bracket, joining the "haves." Coming from less than makes them yearn to buy all the things they wish they could have afforded, filling a void they may not realize they had.

The problem is, spenders frequently have trouble saving money and controlling their debt. Overconsumption of goods is habitual, so they use borrowed money (e.g., credit cards) to feed the habit. Since they use all their excess monthly funds on purchasing, they don't prepare for the future by building savings. This can go on until something happens in their life that triggers a change in behavior.

Having a spending characteristic is most detrimental when it negatively impacts the family. Someone who has a problem with impulse buying can and typically will pass down their habits to their offspring. Left unchecked, this can create generations of learned overspending.

The Saver

Typically, a saver is someone who believes that money is a means to an end, the end being whatever goal they've created. This person will work diligently to achieve their goals, even if it seems unattainable.

For example, if, at their current income, a goal of saving $500 is not reachable, a saver will figure out a way to increase income or cut back on hobbies just to make that goal work. Because they're hyper-focused on this end, they sometimes find it difficult to treat themselves, be generous to others, or even purchase essential items. As a result, they often miss out on many valuable life experiences.

The best thing about a saver, though, is that your money is always safe with them. So, if you are a person who struggles with keeping money in your savings account because you have too much access to it, having an accountability partner who is better at saving would be beneficial.

The Security Seeker

A person who thrives only when they have a cemented place in their family, career, faith, and/or community is a security seeker. From the outside, they may seem like they overthink or focus too much on themselves, but usually, they're seeking security for not only themselves but also for the people close to them. They may have difficulty seizing the moment because, for them, doing well means doing well for everyone. In order to reach this goal, a security seeker is strategic in all money matters.

The challenge for the security seeker is that they take very few risks. Even if it's just a perceived threat, not an actual one, they will steer clear of anything that could impact their forward progress.

A security seeker's personal and professional relationships might also suffer, since they often don't have the capacity to strive for financial greatness and nurture relationships. As a result, building a family later in life might be a better fit.

The Risk Taker

A risk taker is someone who doesn't believe in slowing down and taking time to think; instead, they enjoy taking leaps.

They're comfortable making quick decisions and are bold, decisive, and confident when choosing investments with a high potential for return. However, they get bored easily and are always waiting for the next big idea, and that impatience can cause them to overlook threats or issues with an investment.

Because of this, a risk taker must try to balance freely making money decisions and intuitively understanding which investments will yield the most return. They may also look for longer-term investments if they feel the return is exponential.

The Flyer

A flyer is someone who "flies by the seat of their pants." They have a hands-off approach to their finances, sometimes leading to living beyond their means—even if they make a decent salary.

I know what you're thinking. *How can someone have a surplus and still live beyond their means?* Lack of planning. Because they're hands-off, flyers rarely check up on their financial health. They may even have someone else handling their day-to-day expenses.

All a flyer knows is that the money goes into their account and is available when they want to use it. They don't concern themselves with the who, what, when, where, and how. If they don't have a reputable person/entity managing their funds, they may be susceptible to being taken advantage of.

If it's not clear by now, all spending characteristics are learned, and everyone gravitates toward one or more of these characteristics at different points in life. The twenty-year-old you might be a risk taker while the forty-year-old you is a security seeker, for example. But no matter what, our financial decisions are our responsibility. That's why it's so important to take ownership of our financial education.

What Now?

As we've just discussed, we don't do anything without first learning from our parents, teachers, friends, and, yes, even television. But our parents can only teach us what they know or have experienced, teachers can only teach what is allowed under their curriculum, our friends know just as much or as little as we do, and television can easily be manipulated to promote any narrative.

Fortunately, what we've learned from our daily environment is not all we'll ever know; instead, we can choose to seek knowledge from subject matter experts. People who want to help us achieve our goals. Financial education is no different.

Lack of financial education puts individuals at a disadvantage as adults, so it's time to commit to learning basic principles, common mistakes, and strategies that will positively impact your financial future. Let's start with understanding financial institutions.

Something to Think About...

What spending characteristic(s) have you previously exhibited? What about currently?

Why do you think you have adopted these characteristics at various points in your life?

Do you want to change these characteristics, or are you happy with the status quo?

CHAPTER 2

Understanding Financial Institutions

I have always been a worker. Multiple jobs at that. So, when an opportunity to work full-time at a credit union was presented to me, I applied immediately. After my interview, I was hired pretty much on the spot.

At nineteen, I had no idea what working as a teller would entail, but I had clerical experience that I figured would help me do the job well. Still, I was surprised to see how much detail goes into working with people and their money. The first thing I learned is the industry takes security very seriously. I underwent an extensive background check, along with being bonded.

Before interacting with actual customers, I went through extensive training on the rules that govern financial institutions, including how to prevent fraud and how to process transactions. There, I learned the difference between savings, checking, money market accounts, and certificate of deposits. I learned there were more than three hundred different credit unions in our region that we serviced.

The credit union was also my first introduction to the spending habits we discussed in Chapter 1. I saw, for instance, how people who had overdrawn accounts with a consistently negative balance would have poor credit scores. And how, if those accounts were sent to collections, those same people couldn't open an account anywhere else until they took care of the balance owed.

That's one of many reasons why it's crucial that you understand how financial institutions operate. Only then can you best utilize their services.

How Do I Choose a Financial Institution?

Helping young people protect their finances is a soft spot of mine. Especially because I have witnessed countless minor accounts become unmanageable once the child reaches the "age of maturation."

Minor savings accounts are accounts set up for a child under the age of sixteen, which a parent or guardian manages until the child reaches a certain age. At that time, the account can be converted into a checking account, and the parent or guardian no longer has access to it. This independence is mesmerizing for a teenager, so of course when they're provided with a debit card, their excitement overrides their inquisitiveness about how a checking account works. Too often, their monies dwindle away quickly, and they incur bank fees. The unsuspecting teenager finds themselves in a deficit before even beginning to build.

Similarly, I've witnessed many young adults end up in poor financial situations after aging out of college student checking accounts. These accounts are free for students ages eighteen to twenty-four (ages may vary from institution to institution), but there is no conversation or notice when the account changes. When the account holder no longer meets the criteria for free student checking, the account automatically rolls over into a checking account with a minimum $100 monthly maintenance fee.

In my banking positions, I longed to tell young account holders about accounts offered at other institutions that would better fit their current situation, but I couldn't because it is against policy to offer any suggestions unrelated to the bank you represent. So, I had compassion for them by explaining the true nature of different accounts.

No longer bound by the rules of corporate America, I will now explain the differences between banks and credit unions so you can identify the best financial institution for your current situation. Let's get started.

Credit Unions Versus Banks

Because they're nonprofit, the sole purpose of credit unions is to put members in the best financial situation. They do this by delivering great customer service and providing financial products on the most favorable terms they can afford to offer.

To this end, credit unions have low minimum account opening deposits. In other words, you can open a savings account with a credit union for as little as $5. That low amount makes you a member, giving you access to the same perks (e.g., small dividends, discounted loan rates, minimal or no monthly fees) as someone with $100,000.

However, many credit unions require you to be affiliated with a specific company or organization. The Navy Federal Credit Union, for instance, is for current and/or retired military personnel and their immediate families only. Without proving your relationship with the required party or organization, you will not be able to open an account with the credit union.

Some credit unions, though, have open enrollment. Using their large member base as leverage, they partner with auto insurance, life insurance, and retail companies to offer members the best rates they can.

Banks, meanwhile, are for-profit institutions that offer accounts to almost anyone but large dividends to only a small group of account owners. For example, banks also partner with retailers to offer discounts to customers, but customers often only gain those perks if they have a $25,000 minimum savings balance or if their credit card balance is high enough to earn points.

That said, banks are known for being leaders in technology, and they offer multiple locations per region for customers to enjoy. They have sizable ATM networks that customers can access locally and across the country, and federally insured banks even offer deposit account protection for their customers who have balances up to $250,000. (Credit union funds are also insured, backed by the NCUA—the National Credit Union Administration.)

With digital banking at the forefront of the financial industry, there's been a rise in online banks. Strictly online banks typically offer higher interest rates on products than traditional banks, but they do offer more consumer-friendly options. For example, Chime offers accounts with fewer fees because they have less overhead.

Online banks are ideal for a generation that is used to the ease of digital transactions. They're also great for people who frequently travel. But be careful to avoid offers that seem too good to be true, such as the ever-popular "get your paycheck two days early" program or daily advances on direct deposit checks. On the surface, these offers appear to have convenience for their customers in mind, but they're actually perpetuating the "need it right now" culture and promoting a life of debt management.

Yes, I said debt management. If you are constantly borrowing before you get paid, you will find yourself always trying to get out of the hole. (Food for thought: If they allow you to get your money two days early on Wednesday instead of Friday, aren't you still waiting two weeks to get paid?)

Now that you know which financial institutions you should explore, you need to determine where, specifically, to put your money. To start, consider proximity. Having continued access to money you are trying to save could prove counterproductive, but having a financial institution close to your home or job is helpful when you need face-to-face service.

If you're new to saving money, I suggest prioritizing a little distance and not getting an ATM card for your savings account. Doing these things makes withdrawing money more of a hassle. If you do this, be sure to have the amount you want to save directly deposited into the account instead of having to drop the cash off in person. The less contact you have with your savings account, the better.

After you've narrowed your focus to a few financial institutions, research the stability of each. Access the financials on their websites (e.g., company growth over the last three to five years, assets, debt and merger information) to see whether trusting them is a smart decision.

Merger information, for instance, is very important because when banks are bought out, the types of products they offer often change. Meaning, your maintenance-free account may change to a regular account with stipulations that you don't meet, which you won't know until you're charged a fee. For obvious reasons, the purchasing bank wants to retain as many customer accounts as possible, so they don't have in-depth discussions with customers about account type changes when the merger happens.

What even is a maintenance-free account? you may be wondering. Don't worry, we're going to go over the most common types of accounts next.

Types of Accounts

When choosing a financial institution, it's also important to consider what you need an account *for*. After all, different institutions have different requirements for each type.

The four main types of accounts:

1. **Savings:** This type of account is used to reach a goal (e.g., a car, vacation, college, emergencies), *not* for daily transactions. Savings accounts are limited to six withdrawals per month; if you withdraw more often than that, the bank will change your account type to checking…automatically. Savings account parameters are federally regulated and cannot be changed.

2. **Checking:** This type of account is used for daily transactions. Bill payments and purchases are its main function.
3. **Certificate of Deposit:** This type of savings account locks your interest rate for a period of time. Currently, the minimum deposit for a CD is $500, and the shortest term before you can withdraw money without penalty is nine months.
4. **Money Market Account:** This type of savings account is unique because it includes check writing privileges. These checks can be used to pay for things without counting toward the federally regulated six withdrawals per month. Money market accounts are attractive to high balance carrying customers because they get a tiered interest rate on the account, as well as perks for being valued customers.

If you are looking for a way to pay bills, then a checking account is the way to go. I suggest researching an account that has low account maintenance fees and no minimum balance, since this account will more than likely have a low balance at the end of each month.

You should also try to get an account that doesn't have stipulation for being free. For example, most banks offer a free account if you set up direct deposit, but what if your job doesn't use direct deposit for some reason that month? Or what if you switch jobs and don't get a direct deposit right away? You will still be charged a fee for not meeting the account requirements, and you will be obligated to pay it.

Finally, when choosing an account, think about your current life status. Don't choose an account that has a minimum maintenance balance of $1,000, for example, if you know your account will zero out each month. Even if you are planning on reaching that monthly balance in the future.

There is nothing wrong with starting where you are now and upgrading as your lifestyle changes. In fact, that is the best option for saving yourself time and money.

Number of Accounts

Millions of people have only one checking account for both saving money and paying bills. Although a common practice, this can be dangerous.

First, one account puts you, the consumer, at a greater risk for fraud. If your only account becomes compromised, and the bank has to block your card/account, you won't be able to access any money while they investigate the wrongdoing. Second, lower interest rates typically accompany checking accounts—unless it's a tiered balance account. So, the benefits of keeping higher balances are lower in a standard checking account. Third, all your money going into one account is not the most efficient way to save for different financial goals. You cannot effectively monitor those goals.

Understanding your risk versus reward ratio when dealing with bank accounts is paramount. So, let's look at more of the advantages and disadvantages of having multiple accounts using the lists below.

Disadvantages of multiple accounts:

- Money spread out

- Traveling to multiple places to make large withdrawals
- Harder to compile documents for loan applications
- Missing out on amenities (i.e., combined balance bonuses)
- Not taking advantage of interest (tiered balance ac count)
- Multiple rules/procedures to understand
- Potentially more maintenance fees
- Different debit cards to keep track of

Advantages of multiple accounts:

- Bargaining power
- Bill pay management (specific account for bills)
- Better tracking of savings goals: vacations, college tuition, home, new furniture, retirement
- Prepare for annual expenses (car insurance, property taxes)
- Prepare for emergencies

Throughout this book, I will touch on money management practices that you can use regardless of the number of accounts you hold. But as with all financial decisions, the number that works best for you won't necessarily be the same as your best friend's. It will depend on your current status and goals, so don't rush to open a new account just yet.

How Do I Use My Account(s)?

The banking industry has pushed us all into using online banking more than going to physical branches. For those of us who have been banking for a long time, the convenience is welcome. But new bankers entering the workforce will have first interactions just like ours…so we must teach them.

Let's say you've just received your first check from your first job. You've already opened an account, but as you're attempting to cash your check, the teller says, "Please negotiate the check."

Now this simply means to sign your name on the back of the check…in cursive. (With few exceptions, print is not acceptable.) But if you're banking for the first time, you might not know.

This book is meant to remove some of the anxiety first-time bankers experience, as well as help more experienced bankers fine-tune their knowledge. So, let's begin by discussing what a check is and how it's used.

Checks

A check is a written agreement that a bank will send a specified person or entity a certain amount of money from the maker's account. Once the check is cashed, the terms are final.

The six parts of a check:

1. **Date:** Can be the current date or a future date (this is called *postdated*). If a maker knows the funds for a check won't be available until a certain date, they may postdate it, and the receiver won't be able to cash the check until that date.
2. **Payee:** The person(s) or entity the check is payable to. If a check is made out to two people, both must sign the check on the back and be present to cash it—unless the check is being deposited into a joint account shared by the payees.

3. **Amount:** Written out in words and numerals on the check. The written amount takes precedence over the numerical amount, so be sure they show the exact same thing.
4. **Maker's Signature:** The person writing the check must sign it on the front bottom right.
5. **Financial Institution:** Bank the account is drawn on. You may cash checks at your bank, or you may take the check to the bank it is drawn on and cash it for a small fee. The drawn-on bank will try to get you to open an account if you cash it as a noncustomer of theirs, but don't feel pressured; you don't have to open an account to cash the check.
6. **MICR Encoding Numbers:** The numbers at the bottom of the check that represent the account number, routing number, and check number. These must be present for the check to be cashed.

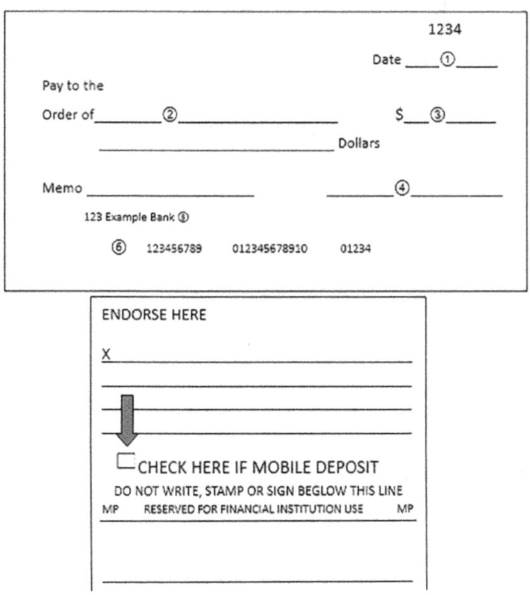

It's important to fill everything out because checks with blanks on them can either get rejected or be cashed by anyone. Also remember that changing anything on a check you did not write is considered altering a check and is a type of fraud.

New checking accounts used to receive a starter book of checks but now you must specifically request to order checks for your account at a fee. Some financial institutions will offer you free over the counter checks to use while you wait for your checks to come in the mail, and others may offer you a complimentary cashier's check for immediate use. But while there was an era of bankers who only wrote checks, today most account holders use debit cards for everyday purchases.

Debit Cards

Debit cards are the electronic version of a check. Nothing more, nothing less. But unlike checks, they are given to you for free when you open a checking account. And they're much more efficient because of the EFT (electronic funds transfer) process, which enables the requesting bank to confirm the availability of funds immediately.

When you're issued a debit card, the bank will send you a randomly assigned Personal Identification Number (PIN) in the mail. You input this PIN whenever you try to access the money in your account, whether using an ATM or making a purchase in the store. You can change your PIN anytime to whatever number you want, but I recommend not using a number associated with you or your family. (I actually just use the random PIN the bank assigns me.)

Note that debit cards *can* be used without a PIN, but doing so automatically makes it a credit transaction, and the account will be debited $1 to ensure the account is open and valid. When the retailer closes their credit card machine at the end of the night, the customer will see the amount of their purchase as a pending debit from their account. The retailer has one to three business days to charge their account, or the pending charge will fall off.

It can take a while for a check to be mailed and money to be cleared from an account, so people who were not diligent about tracking their checks would sometimes write checks based on an available balance that hadn't been updated. In other words, they were double spending, causing the account to be overdrawn. Debit card use can help customers avoid overdraft fees by more easily tracking their transactions and showing real-time updated balances.

Interestingly, debit cards were popularized to minimize bank loss due to check fraud and checks not clearing. But while electronic processing of checks has decreased check clearing loss, it has not eliminated all threats. According to the 2024 Abrigo Fraud Survey, 61 percent of Americans still write checks. An ABA Banking Journal article reports that checks are the second-most-common form of payments for values exceeding $500. Despite a decline in overall check volume over the years, incidents of fraud and the resulting losses remain high. (Rector, 2025)

Account Management

Online banking, including the use of mobile banking apps, has made managing money easier—at least for those who value convenience banking. In this section, I will share some key features on most electronic banking platforms, which can aid in securing your financial future. These features help with either maintenance or planning. (I call them Nurture or Future, since your financial health is a cycle of being able to maintain what you have while preparing for what's next.)

Common maintenance features:

- The **account activity** and **monthly statement** tabs enable you to verify processed and pending transactions and see your available spending balance.
- Using **direct deposits** and **mobile check deposits** saves you time by efficiently getting money into your account. (While direct deposit may seem like a small feature because every business offers it, not having it can result in untracked spending.)
- **Overdraft options**, typically available via online banking, give you the chance to opt out of allowing transactions to be processed if you don't have enough available balance, helping you avoid overdraft fees. These convenience fees are usually around $35, which may seem negligible but can add up quickly. (Overdraft Protection (ODP) requires much discipline and the understanding that you are essentially borrowing from the bank.)
- **Rewards programs** ensure you are maximizing the benefits of your account. (Most financial institutions have an earnings program that gives you points for everyday debit card purchases, which you can redeem for items from participating retailers or funds deposited into an eligible account.)

Using these online features will help you understand your current account status.

Common planning features:

- **Budgeting and saving tools** enable you to see your entire financial picture in one place. Often, they enable you to choose a start date, target date (when you want to reach the goal), and amount; you get to see your entire financial picture with that institution all in one place.
- Monitoring **interest rates** helps you assess your ability to take advantage of potential savings available during the life of your loan. For example, in some instances, having a rate/term refinance can lower your monthly payments, as well as reduce the interest cost over the life of the loan. Lowered monthly payments result in extra money, which can be allocated to other financial goals.
- Assigning a **beneficiary** allows you to state who can access your account after presenting your death certificate. (Beneficiaries should not be confused with joint account holders; joint account holders already have access to the funds and enjoy the same benefits as the primary account holder.) Having a beneficiary in place prevents your account from being absorbed by the bank upon your death, as well as guarantees your loved ones receive an inheritance.
- Remember, all financial institutions have features, programs, and recommended strategies for helping you manage your money and reach your financial goals. We will dive more deeply into some of these, like setting goals and creating spending

plans, later on, but for now, think about how you are currently using financial tools and whether they are working the way you need them to.

Where Do I Begin?

Armed with this new information, I'm sure you are very excited to look at your accounts with a different lens. To examine your account structure and determine if you are using your accounts to the maximum benefit available to you.

At this time, you should be asking yourself, *Am I using the accounts that best serve me at my current financial status? Do I have enough accounts to match the financial goals I have set in place?*

Whether you have two or ten accounts to separate your family's financial goals, the choice is up to you. No two financial plans for success will look the same. Just remember to consider proximity when choosing a brick-and-mortar-based financial institution for your savings accounts. Consider the stability of the institution you are partnering with. Nothing is guaranteed because financial changes in business can happen at any time, but putting yourself in the best position possible initially will warrant success more often.

Something to Think About...

How did you choose your current financial institution?

How many accounts do you currently have? List them.

Is this setup working for you? Why or why not?

CHAPTER 3

Taking on Debt

Coming from a family of accounting professionals, my adolescence was filled with talks about education and the workforce. Numbers were at the forefront of every conversation. Yet I was not enthused about going to college straight after high school, despite my interest in computer science and technology. In fact, I had no interest in enrolling until a good friend convinced me to take the entrance test for Marygrove College.

At seventeen, I was able to register myself for classes and sign up for financial aid. I was told that due to my mother's income, I should qualify for some awards and grants. The rest of my tuition I could pay for with student loans.

This didn't concern me. At the time, I was too focused on *How do I get these classes done?* Besides, my understanding, based on conversations in my home, was that the only way to finish college was to get student loans.

Once the loans were applied to my account, I seemed to always have an excess. It seemed like a blessing as I worked through college, but what I didn't know was there would be ramifications for taking extra money. That they would have compounding interest.

Not only that, but I also took out loans for three semesters before I understood that I did not have to take everything that was offered to me. I could mitigate my debt by accepting only what I needed to cover my current class load.

Upon graduating, I didn't initially secure a job in my industry and didn't immediately make the income I anticipated. So, when the payment requests began showing up from my student loan servicer, I did what many do. I paid them until I didn't.

That's right. When I didn't have the funds, I just ignored the requests. Eventually, I realized I had options for paying back the debt, but by then, my credit score had been negatively impacted. (Credit is an agreement between a lender and borrower that goods or services that are obtained before payment will be paid in the future, often with interest.)

This scenario is not uncommon, especially because many people grow up with beliefs like "Loans are free money," "Debt is normal," and "You're going to die owing someone, so there's no need to pay off all your debt." But ignoring debt doesn't make it disappear; it only heightens your anxiety and prolongs the inevitable. That's why you must learn how to responsibly take on and manage your debt.

But Isn't Some Debt Good?

Consumers obtain debt to reach a desired goal, like education. My story exemplifies how student loans seem inevitable when parents don't prepare early and/or students don't work hard for awards and grants. In fact, 80 percent of students who receive a bachelor's degree have education debt by the time they graduate. (Hanson 2024)

This is far from the only kind of debt. Traditional credit includes any trade line that is reported to a repository or bureau, impacting your credit score. Common trade line types are major credit cards, revolving accounts, secured credit cards, auto loans/lease, mortgages, installment accounts, and personal and student loans, to name a few. The credit lines shown on your report are used to exhibit creditworthiness to lenders.

New credit applicants may run into a roadblock when attempting to obtain a loan if no credit history or score is available at the time of the application. In certain circumstances, underwriters can allow non-traditional credit lines to be used in an effort to approve the loan. Examples of acceptable nontraditional credit lines include utility payments, proof of rental income or insurance payments, repayment of personal debt, lot rent for mobile home, and childcare or child support payments. Providing proof of consistently paying debts is what lenders want to see.

Now, some people argue that home loans and auto loans are "good debt," but I'm here to tell you, there is no such thing. Obtaining debt is simply a means to an end, one that requires careful consideration and planning. We'll talk about a few types of credit in more detail next.

Home Loans

Let's say you want to own property to realize the "American dream" but don't have enough liquid assets to purchase one. You decide to take on a traditional home loan but aren't sure how much you can realistically afford. Let me take a moment to give you a brief overview of how banks qualify you.

Lenders take risks when they lend money. For this reason, they want to be sure you can make your house payments. There are limits on your monthly debt allowance based on your gross monthly income. These limits are called ratios, and they are used by underwriters to make a decision on whether to lend to you.

The **housing ratio** is used to determine how much of your gross monthly income can be used toward a mortgage payment. Generally, this ratio is 25 to 33 percent of your gross monthly income. Below is the formula used:

Gross monthly income x housing ratio (%) = maximum house payment

As an example, let's say a potential homebuyer's gross monthly income is $4,000. If they put 33 percent of their income toward mortgage payments, they could afford a home with a maximum monthly payment of $1,320.

However, when deciding to move forward, you can't just stop at how much house you can afford. You must also look at other monthly financial obligations.

To that end, lenders next consider your **debt-to-income ratio** (DTI). In other words, your potential monthly mortgage payment plus all your existing monthly debt payments, such as car/personal loans or credit cards. Lenders like to see this ratio between 36 and 43 percent, using the following formula:

Maximum payment for housing + existing debts ÷ gross monthly income = Debt to Income Ratio

Let's build on the previous example. The potential homebuyer makes $200 monthly payments on their credit card, so the lender adds that to their maximum mortgage payment ($1,320) to get $1,520. They then divide that expense by their gross monthly income ($4,000). They determine that the homebuyer's DTI ratio is 0.38, or 38 percent. Because the potential homebuyer is within the preferred housing and DTI ratios, the lender will likely decide to move forward with the loan.

It's important to remember that lenders determine your eligibility using the debts on your credit report, not additional expenses like daycare payments or school tuition or the $300/month you give to help your parents out. They don't factor in utility payments that you'll be making on a new home. Not only all that, but also your DTI is determined based on your *gross* monthly income instead of your net income (the amount you actually take home after taxes).

I encourage you to use the DTI formula yourself, plugging in your net income, debt payments, and additional expenses. The results may shock you. By showing and offering you a home on the higher end of your budget—maybe $300,000 when in fact you can only afford a home that's $200,000 according to all of your expenses—lenders may even try to make you think that there is no home in your budget that you'll be happy with. But let me assure you: You can always find a home that works once your expectations meet reality. Plus, determining your own maximum house payment will give you the confidence to advocate for yourself when a lender attempts to put you in a home that costs more than you can afford.

Auto Loans

A vehicle is a depreciating asset, meaning the value decreases as soon as you take it off the lot. Even if you pay full price for the vehicle, in most cases, you won't ever get that investment back—and if you get a loan for it, you'll actually pay *more* than its value over time. So, the best way to avoid unnecessary costs is to build up your savings and purchase your vehicle with cash.

Since leasing or buying a car is inevitable for most people, I want to arm you with actions to take. These fall within three categories: Plan to Shop, Negotiating, Closing the Deal.

When planning to shop, budget wisely. Check your credit report so you know your spending limits ahead of time. If you're caught off by your score, the salesperson may try to take advantage of your vulnerability and offer you a less-than-favorable deal.

It's important to know that checking your credit with multiple lenders negatively impacts your score. So, if you are actively shopping, have all the lenders check your credit within a fourteen-day time span so that the inquiries only impact your score once. (Credit bureaus understand rate shopping; they won't ding you if they see multiple inquires within two weeks.)

As a rule of thumb, don't let anyone check your score until you have done all of your initial research and are ready to purchase. This includes thinking about add-ons you might want and finding out how much they cost, checking current auto loan rates, and getting pre-approved from auto-financing sources (your bank or credit union) that are not used by the dealerships. You should also decide if you want or need a cosigner who can help you navigate the new situation and ease some of the stress. Finally, if you're trading in a vehicle, research its approximate value beforehand instead of just trusting the value the salesperson tells you.

Once you're ready to purchase, know how to negotiate. Most people think that once a salesperson presents you with an itemized list of payments, the deal is complete. On the contrary, you can negotiate the annual percentage rate (APR) and interest rate, the length of the loan, whether or not there will be a pre-payment penalty, and any additional fees associated with the loan. You can also negotiate optional products (e.g., warranties, gap insurance), as well as optional physical features, the down payment amount, dealer fees/origination fees, and the trade-in amount. This is why I say knowing the value of your trade-in vehicle ahead of time is helpful; it arms you with knowledge in case the salesperson's offer doesn't match up. If you don't know what it's worth, how can you negotiate?

Many people choose longer loan terms because they allow you to pay less each month, but you end up paying more interest over time. Shorter loan terms reduce your total loan cost, and a higher down payment or higher price for your trade-in can reduce it further. Remember to negotiate a lower total cost, not just a lower monthly payment; getting a lower interest rate and APR will help with this, preventing you from having negative equity.

Negotiation isn't the final step, however. When closing the deal, read the disclosures and verify that the terms are what you agreed to. This includes the APR (the cost of credit in a percentage) and finance charge (the cost of credit in a dollar amount)—in other words, the interest and fees paid over the life of the loan. Then finish the paperwork, ensuring all copies are signed by you and the dealer with no blank spots. If something isn't right, walk away.

I know seeing "walk away" in this discussion on closing the deal section seems off. But I want you to understand that you as the consumer have rights. If any aspect of the deal doesn't feel right or look right, no one can force you to sign. You can walk away from the deal for any reason prior to signing.

If all goes well and you walk away with a vehicle you love and can afford, your next step is to wait for the intro message from the lender and make your payments on time.

Credit Cards

As soon as you turn eighteen, Visa, Mastercard, Discover, and American Express, to name a few, begin to court you. I say "court" because it is a song and dance, one that gets many consumers into deep debt.

The purpose of credit card companies is to get you to spend money you don't have so that they can earn interest from it. The marketing tactics they use are simple. Offer you "points" to use in the future and entice you with impulse buying power. Enable you to live a lifestyle you cannot afford with your current cash flow.

Let me warn you: You will never beat the credit card company. They always win! If you think you are going to trick them by earning the points and avoiding paying interest, well, good luck with that. Credit card companies are good at keeping you in debt because of how interest is calculated.

Simple interest is a set percentage paid on the initial principal. So, if you borrowed $1,000 and agreed to pay it back three years later at 20 percent annual interest, then you would owe $600 in interest, plus the $1,000 you borrowed.

If you had a $1,000 loan with interest that compounded 20 percent annually, you would owe 20 percent on the annual balance, which would increase every year with the addition of that year's interest. After three years, you would owe $1,728—$1,000 in principal and $728 in interest.

Most loans don't compound annually but instead use a daily, weekly, or monthly increment. Credit cards, for example, compound daily. As an informed consumer, you must know what your interest rate is, when your statement cycle ends and begins, and of course your due date. All of these things can be found in your credit card app or on your statement.

See the sample credit card statement below for need-to-know information.

Account Summary	**04/12/2021 - 05/11/2021**
Previous Balance	$648.19
Payments and Credits	-$58.19
Purchases	+$0.00
Balance Transfers	+$0.00
Cash Advances	+$0.00
Fees Charged	+$0.00
Interest Charged	+$0.00
New Balance:	**$590.00**

See Interest Charge Calculation section following the Fees and Interest Charged section for detailed APR information

Credit Line	$5,500
Credit Line Available	$4,910
Cash Advance Credit Line	$2,800
Cash Advance Credit Line Available	$2,800

FICO® Score 8 based on TransUnion® data:

824 Exceptional — **AS OF 05/05/21** Updated Monthly

See Key Factors that help explain your score at Discover.com or visit our mobile app

Payment Information

New Balance	Minimum Payment	Payment Due Date
$590.00	**$35.00**	**06/06/2021**

Late Payment Warning: If we do not receive your minimum payment by the date listed above, you may have to pay a late fee of up to $40.00.

Minimum Payment Warning: If you make only the minimum payment each period, you will pay more in interest and it will take longer to pay off your balance. For example:

If you make no additional charges using this card and each month you pay...	You will pay off the balance shown on this statement in about...	And you will end up paying an estimated total of...
Only the minimum payment	19 months	$596

If you would like information about credit counseling services, call us at 1-800-347-1121.

Refer a Friend

Get a statement credit

Refer a friend to Discover and you can each get a statement credit when they get a card.*

Go to Discover.com/sharediscover87

Payments. You may pay all or part of your Account balance at any time. However, you must pay at least the Minimum Payment Due by the Payment Due Date. Send only your allowable form of payment ("Payment") and the bottom portion of this statement in the envelope provided, after affixing postage. Payments sent without proper postage will be returned to the sender. If you pay by check, you authorize us to use information on your check to make an electronic fund transfer from your account at the financial institution indicated on your check or to process the payment as a check transaction. If a Payment is processed as an electronic fund transfer, the transfer will be for the amount of the check, funds may be withdrawn from your account as soon as the same day we receive your check, and you will not receive your check back.

Please do not send cash. Sending cash is not allowed. The processing of your allowable form of Payment may be delayed if you send cash or correspondence with your Payments, if you send the Payment to any other address, or if you use an envelope other than the one provided. Payments received at our processing facility by 5PM local time on any day will be credited to your Account as of that day. Payments received at our processing facility after 5PM local time will be credited to your Account as of the next day. If you have misplaced your envelope, send your Payment to Discover, PO Box 6103, Carol Stream, IL 60197-6103. Please allow 7-10 days for delivery. If your Payment is returned unpaid, we reserve the right to resubmit it as an electronic debit. **Payments made online or by phone before Midnight Eastern Time on any day except your Statement Closing Date will be credited as of the same day; on your Statement Closing Date, online and phone payments must be made before 5:00 PM Eastern Time to be credited as of that day.**

You can also make a Payment or set up automatic payments by calling 1-800-347-2683. Automatic payments for the billing period shown on your statement will be deducted on the Payment Due Date shown on that statement, or the next automatic payment date referred to on your statement, unless you request a recurring payment date that occurs before your Payment Due Date. In order to schedule monthly payments by telephone, you will need this statement and your bank account information. You will be asked to provide the last four (4) digits of the social security number of the primary borrower as your electronic signature. By providing those numbers, you will be agreeing to this authorization to allow us and your bank to deduct each payment you authorize, in the amount selected by you, from your bank account. You also authorize us to initiate debit or credit entries to your bank account, as applicable, to correct an error in the processing of such payment. You can cancel or modify a payment from your bank account until 5:00 PM Eastern Time on the day such payment is scheduled by calling 1-800-347-2683 or by mail at Discover, PO Box 30421, Salt Lake City, UT 84130-0421. Same day online or phone payments from bank account made after 5:00 PM Eastern Time may be modified before Midnight Eastern Time of that day. Payments from Cashback Bonus cannot be modified or cancelled after being made or scheduled.

○ Full Pay ____________________ ○ Min Pay ____________________
○ Min Pay+ $____________________ ○ Other Amount $ ____________________
Bank Routing #____
Bank Account #____
Monthly on the ○ Payment Due Date, or ○ _____ Day of the month (INSERT DATE)

Credit Reporting. Credit Reporting. We may report information about your Account to credit bureaus. Late payments, missed payments, or other defaults on your Account may be reflected in your credit report. We normally report the status and payment history of your Account to credit reporting agencies each month. If you believe that our report is inaccurate or incomplete, please write us at this address: Discover, PO Box 30939, Salt Lake City, UT 84130-0939. Please include your name, address, home telephone number and Account number.

Paying Interest. Your due date is at least 25 days after the close of each billing period (at least 23 days for billing periods that begin in February). We will begin charging interest on Cash Advances and Balance Transfers as of the later of the Transaction Date or the first day of the billing period in which the transaction posted to your Account. If you pay the New Balance on your current billing statement by the Payment Due Date shown on that billing statement, we will not impose interest charges on New Purchases. New Purchases are Purchases that first appear on the next billing statement. Interest will continue to accrue each day on purchases that appeared on previous billing statements until you pay the New Balance in full and will be billed in the next billing cycle.

How We Calculate Interest Charges. We Use the Daily Balance Method (including current transactions) to calculate the Balance Subject to Interest Rate. For more information, please call us at 1-800-347-2683.

Balance Subject To Interest Rate. Your statement shows a Balance Subject to Interest Rate. It shows this for each transaction category. The Balance Subject to Interest Rate is the average of the daily balances during the billing period.

Credit Balances. If your Account has a credit balance, the amount is shown on the front of your billing statement. A credit balance is money that is owed to you. You may make charges against this amount if your Account is open. We will send you a refund of any remaining balance of $1.00 or more after 6 months, or as otherwise required by applicable law, or upon request made to the address in the Contact Us section on page 3 of your billing statement.

Balance Transfers. Balance Transfers are offered at our discretion and accrue interest at the standard purchase rate unless we tell you otherwise.

Fees and Interest Charged

TOTAL FEES FOR THIS PERIOD	**$0.00**
TOTAL INTEREST FOR THIS PERIOD	**$0.00**
2021 TOTALS YEAR-TO-DATE CHARGED	**AMOUNT**
TOTAL FEES CHARGED IN 2021	$18.60
TOTAL INTEREST CHARGED IN 2021	$0.00

Interest Charge Calculation

Your Annual Percentage Rate (APR) is the annual interest rate on your account.

CURRENT BILLING PERIOD: 30 DAYS

TYPE OF BALANCE	APR*	PROMO APR EXPIRES**	BALANCE SUBJECT TO INTEREST RATE	INTEREST CHARGE
Purchases	0.00%	04/11/22	$7.36	$0.00
Cash Advances	24.99% V	N/A	$0.00	$0.00
Balance Transfers	0.00%	05/11/22	$627.25	$0.00

V = VARIABLE RATE

* If your account is currently enrolled in a special program or is placed into one during the term of the offer, you will receive the benefit of the lower rate while the special program is in effect. This includes, if applicable, any lower rates as authorized under the Servicemembers Civil Relief Act.

** This is the date your promotional rate expires and the remaining balance will be moved to your standard APR disclosed when you accepted the offer. Please note: Changing your payment due date may change your Promo APR Expiration Date.

*** For more information, please call us at 1-800-347-2683.

Now that you know what information to look for and where to find it, take a little time to go over your credit card statements to make sure you know all you need to know about your card.

Statistically speaking, at some point, you will use the credit card for something that you deem an emergency and you will not be able pay that balance off immediately. For example, an unexpected medical expense is a worthy credit card purchase. In fact, using your credit card for this type of large expense is often cheaper than using provider-offered financing options.

When faced with large, unexpected expenses, call your credit card company and ask for two things: a credit line increase and a better repayment plan. Say that you're considering using the provider-offered financing, since no credit card company wants to hear that you are thinking about spending your money elsewhere. Generally, both requests will be granted, giving you an increased credit limit and a lower interest rate on purchases for a period of time.

One caveat: Do not call asking for a credit line increase if you are not in good standing and/or if your card is at its limit. Credit bureaus want your credit utilization ratio—the amount of credit you've used divided by your limit—to be no more than 30 percent. Why? Keeping high balances appears to creditors as an inability to pay.

For example, if your balance is $450 and your credit limit is $650, your current utilization is 69 percent. A utilization that high needs to be paid down as soon as possible in order to put your credit score back in good standing.

It's human nature to use a credit card if it's available, so the best way to avoid temptation is to not have one at all. But since that is an unrealistic expectation, it is better that we understand how to use a credit card responsibly.

So, How Can I Responsibly Manage My Debt?

The main benefit of debt—whether from a loan or credit card—is that it helps you establish credit, which you can use to make large purchases. Good credit essentially tells lenders that you can be trusted to pay back borrowed debt.

Having good credit affords you the luxury of a lower interest rate. That lower interest rate makes it easier to pay your note on time, positively impacting your credit score. But if you don't already have good credit, your interest rate will be higher, meaning it will cost you more money in the long run *for the same amount of borrowed money.*

Why? Companies believe people with higher credit scores will pay their bills on time, so they will get their profit—the interest—on time as well. In contrast, they view people with lower credit scores as a risk, and because of that perceived risk, they charge those people more interest. I know it seems backwards, but lenders believe people with lower credit scores will not pay their debt on time or in full. The higher interest rate is meant to deter them from not paying what they owe.

So, let's look at how credit scores are calculated, what good credit does for you, how bad credit harms you, and how you can check your credit score. That way, you can responsibly manage any current or future debt.

The Four Cs of Credit

Underwriters determining your creditworthiness look at the four Cs: Capital, Collateral, Capacity, and Character. Let's define each:

- **Capital** refers to the cash reserves you have available to cover expenses like a down payment, loan fees, closing costs, reserves for emergencies, and moving costs.
- **Capacity** speaks to your ability to repay the requested loan amount. To determine this, lenders look at your current income, debt obligations listed on your credit report (used to calculate your debt-to-income ratio), and employment history.
- **Collateral** should be thought of in two ways. First, do you have an asset to forfeit that is the same or higher value than the loan you are trying to obtain? For example, if you use your car as collateral for a personal loan, you forfeit the vehicle in the event that you don't pay the loan back. Second, if you buy a car, the vehicle itself is the collateral that ensures you will pay the loan back.
- **Character** speaks to the history you have of paying your bills. Lenders trust that if you pay other creditors successfully, you will also pay their loan back.

FICO scoring is a credit scoring model that is applied to major purchases like mortgages and auto loans. VANTAGE scores are used for retail credit cards. Although they have similar scoring models, these companies weigh categories differently when determining eligibility.

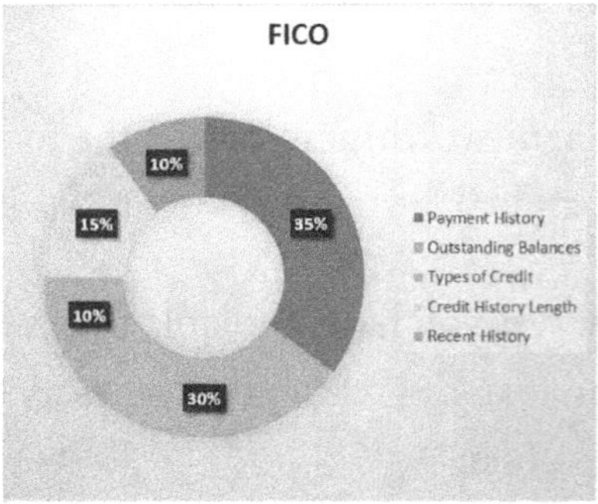

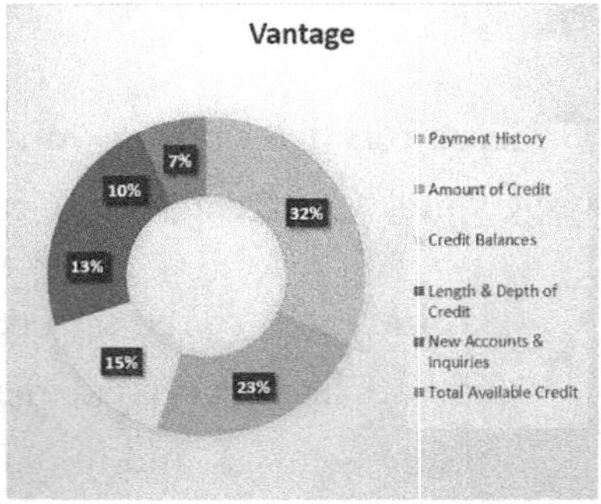

As you can see, payment history makes up 35 percent of your FICO score and 32 percent of your VANTAGE score. So, if you're looking to improve your credit score, the best thing to do is pay your bills on time. You won't see any significant improvements until you start doing this consistently.

The main difference between FICO and VANTAGE scores? VANTAGE scores = retail credit. FICO scores = major credit purchases.

The main thing both scoring models have in common? Payment history is the highest weighted item impacting scores.

Now, we all know people who try to "build their credit" by applying for multiple credit cards. Sometimes their credit card applications are accepted and sometimes not, but either way, they don't understand why their credit score isn't improving. But if you look at the pie chart, having multiple types of credit (e.g., credit cards, home/auto loans) only accounts for 10 percent of your score. What's worse is that if your application is denied, your score is negatively impacted.

But don't fear. Your credit score describes your financial patterns over a period of time…it's not forever! Your financial picture can be changed by focusing on the pie and not the score. Pay your bills on time and keep your outstanding balances in a healthy range, and you can turn bad credit into good credit.

Good Versus Bad Credit

Keeping good credit is a financial strategy that can be used to plan for your future financial success. How? Utilizing the modern credit scoring system in a way that saves you money over time gives you the opportunity to put surplus monies toward financial goals instead of debt reduction.

Let's examine the chart below:

CREDIT SCORE	MORTGAGE RATES $250,000	AUTO LOAN RATES $25,000	INSURANCE RATES	CREDIT CARD RATES
300-550 Poor	9.5% $712,500	18.9% $13,828	HIGHER	28.9%
550-620 Subprime	8.6% $637,500	17.9% $13,009		19.8%
620-680 Acceptable	4.9% $337,500	11% $7,614		13.9%
680-710 Good	4.2% $300,000	6.5% $4,350		12.14%
710-850 Excellent	3.5% $262,500	5.1% $3,375	LOWER	7.99%

This chart describes approximate rates for different loans based on your credit score. For example, a consumer who has a credit score of 600 will pay $637,500 over the life of a $250,000 mortgage loan—$375,000 more than a consumer with a 730 credit score.

Hopefully, this chart does not deter you from making major life choices; after all, buying a car and a home is a sign of independence and a major step into adulthood. My goal is simply to equip you with enough information to make an educated decision when the time comes to spend money.

Good credit allows you to rent or buy things you want, lease favorable properties, establish utility services, obtain insurance at a lower rate, and get lower interest rates generally, enabling you to save more money. So, use the above chart as an incentive to keep your credit in good standing. Debt is the killer of wealth building.

Credit Reports

But what is credit? You may be asking. Credit is the ability of a consumer to obtain goods or services before payment based on the trust that payment will be made in the future.

As we've discussed, credit reports are used by lenders to determine a person's creditworthiness. These reports show your payment history for your mortgage, car loans, credit cards, etc., as recorded using your unique Social Security number (SSN). If an entity requests your credit report, specific personal information will be provided to them, such as your name, address, and date of birth.

Importantly, your credit report shows if any debts are delinquent. They also show public information, such as bankruptcy filings, foreclosures, judgments, and tax liens. Finally, inquiries from lenders or others who have requested your report within the previous two years will show up.

Fortunately, there are many places where you can check your credit score so you can stay abreast of your financial picture. The key is understanding what each platform provides. For example, the following websites allow users to check their FICO credit score:

- Experian.com
- Nerdwallet.com
- CreditJourney.com
- Mint.intuit.com

Another place to get accurate credit scores is inside your credit card app or website. Credit card companies such as Discover, Chime, and American Express all have a tab to view scores; you just need to be a customer of theirs to access this information.

The following sites allow you to register for free credit reports and VANTAGE scores. There is no catch; you do not even have to subscribe or enroll for a trial of anything because these sites make money from advertising:

- CreditKarma.com
- CreditSesame.com
- WalletHub.com

The most reputable site to obtain credit reports is annualcreditreport.com; for example, consumers can obtain one free credit report per year. You will be asked for personal information, but do not be alarmed. This is just so that they can verify your identity.

One benefit of annualcreditreport.com is that it requests reports from agencies like Equifax, Transunion, and Experian in one place. You simply select the bureau you want a report from first, then answer the verifying questions. If those questions match what is on your file with that entity, you will be allowed to view, download, and save your report. You can do this for each agency.

If at any time your identifying information does not match what's in an agency's system, an electronic copy of your report will not be available. You will be given steps on how to obtain a copy of your report via mail. (Annualcreditreport.com does not pull your credit score, but when you're working on improving your credit rating, the current score shouldn't be a concern. The items on the report—your spending characteristics—should be your focus.)

Another way to obtain an up-to-date credit report is to work with local nonprofit organizations. Most have a financial capabilities department that can help coach you to financial success. They can also pull a credit report for you, along with your credit score. Certain services with nonprofit organizations are provided free of charge, so it's a good way to get help while watching your budget.

When going through financial hardship, it's hard to think of anything else but how to get out of it. It's even hard to believe that anyone else can understand what you are going through. However, when it comes to credit issues, you are not alone. No one is perfect. And since your credit score is just a snapshot of a particular time in your life, understand that it won't be like that forever.

The following list details common credit problems that most consumers have or will face at one time or another:

- **Incorrect Reporting/Data:** This is more common than most think. One incorrect number on your SSN or one incorrect letter in the spelling of your name could cause misinformation on your report.

- **Pattern of Late Payments:** Payments are usually reported late or missing at thirty, sixty, and ninety days after they're due.
- **Bankruptcies:** This is a legal action that consumers use as a last resort, either liquidating assets (Chapter 7) or attempting to enter into a payment plan (Chapter 13).
- **Judgments or Liens:** Judgments show up if you lose a court case and are ordered to pay an amount. In addition, a company may put a tax lien on your personal property in an attempt to collect a debt.
- **Collection Accounts:** Accounts can be moved to collection status by a company after a certain amount of time of nonpayment. Specifically, an account shows up on your report as a collection once the company has given up on attempting to collect the debt through their normal collection procedures.
- **Charge-Offs:** These accounts have gone so long without being paid that the creditor has closed their books on them and taken the debt as a loss.
- **Foreclosures or Repossessions:** These are homes or cars that were taken back due to prolonged nonpayment status.

Common credit problems have a standard length of time to be visible on your credit report for potential lenders to see. Although negatively reported items lose their impact to your credibility over time, knowing the impact should help you make conscious decisions.

Look at the following chart on the length of time various credit problems stay on your credit report:

Negative Item	Time on Credit Report
Late Payment History	7 years
General Civil Judgments	7 years from date filed
Tax Liens	7 years from date paid
Collection Accounts	7 years from original default date
Chapter 13 Bankruptcy	10 years from filing date or discharge/dismiss
Chapter 7 Bankruptcy	10 years from discharge/dismiss
Student Loans	7 years after guarantor actions
Inquiries	2 years

Collection accounts, for example, stay on a report for seven years after the original default date. A default date is the day the account becomes delinquent. So, if your payment is due on a thirty-day cycle but you don't pay it until the next day, your default date is Day 31.

Consumers have the right to get an understanding of debts owed and possibly negotiate with creditors, but only under certain circumstances will an item be removed prior to the standing reporting time.

How Do I Fix Errors?

I know what you're thinking. Sometimes there are items reported incorrectly on your report that have nothing to do with how you are managing your money. After all, errors are among the most common credit reporting issues. You may have heard that disputing accounts on your credit report is possible but you don't know how, so let's take the time now to discuss consumer rights.

Consumer Rights Acts

In 1970, the **Fair Credit Reporting Act (FCRA)** was enacted to promote the accuracy, fairness, and privacy of consumer information contained in the files of consumer reporting agencies. Because of this, credit bureaus (e.g., Equifax, Experian, TransUnion) are now required to maintain accurate information.

As a follow-up to FCRA, the **Fair Credit Billing Act (FCBA)** was enacted in 1974 for revolving accounts. This act established procedures for resolving unauthorized charges, including requiring billing statements to be mailed/distributed fourteen days before the due date. It helped and continues to help consumers stay informed, as well as prevents credit companies from collecting unfair late payment fees. With all the potential fraud, it's nice to know we can dispute unauthorized charges without hassle.

Also in 1974, the **Fair and Accurate Credit Transactions Act (FACTA)** was introduced to help protect consumers against identity theft. FACTA does this by making free annual credit reports available to consumers and giving consumers the ability to add fraud alerts to their credit report.

One major change that has since happened—and is so prevalent and normal for consumers now that we may not recognize its significance—is the truncation of important numbers. This means hiding a portion of important information so that it doesn't fall into the wrong hands. For example, when we make purchases today, our receipts only show the last four digits of our card number. Similarly, bank receipts only show the last four to six digits of your account number. When you enter your password or Social Security number online, it shows up as an asterisk for your protection. All these things are part of an effort to protect consumers and keep them informed about their rights.

Now that you know why you are able to fix errors and your right to have accurate information reported about you, let's talk about how to solve your credit problems.

Solutions to Credit Errors

Correcting credit errors consists of disputing reported information, validating accounts, settling reported accounts, and deleting charge-offs. You will most likely use a combination of these strategies, but thanks to technology, you can do so quickly via credit agency websites or mobile apps.

Unfortunately, there are many times when a consumer just can't seem to get a resolution electronically. One reason is that, depending on the debt's account status, there is certain verbiage that you must use to get results.

Let's walk through the steps of getting an account removed from a credit report.

1. **Dispute Errors with Credit Bureaus:** This process is typically done online and is used for correcting inaccurate information on your credit report. For example, your report may show your car loan payment began 2024 when you actually leased it in 2022. You want your report to show as many on-time payments as

possible, and this inaccurate date reduces your credit length history. Disputing can also be used to correct personal information, such as name spelling and Social Security number errors.

2. **Contact the Creditor Directly:** This is one way to find out what you are "accused of." In other words, the amount the creditor claims you owe; the original borrowed amount, date, and account numbers you are being associated with; etc. You can find most of this information in an updated credit report, but if not, a quick phone call to the creditor will provide you what you need.
3. **Send a Validation Letter:** This is the most important step because it represents the "show and prove" portion of the process. You use the information provided to you from the creditor and ask them in writing to prove to you that you incurred this debt. (The verbiage is very precise for this step, so I will provide a template for you at the end of this book.) The burden of proof is on the creditor at this point.
4. **Write a Consumer Statement, if Needed:** Consumer statements can be used to explain your position regarding the reported account. For example, you might write a statement describing how you fell behind on payments because you were hospitalized and weren't able to resume payments until you returned to work. This statement stays on file with the credit bureaus and can sometimes aid in helping a potential lender decide to approve you, especially if you have begun to make timely payments again.
5. **Send a Deletion Letter:** A deletion letter is used in conjunction with a validation letter *only* when you believe an account was opened erroneously. The reason is, when the credit bureaus receive the deletion request from you, they will reach out to

that creditor in an attempt to validate the account. If during the final verification process, the creditor is able to produce original signed documents, the credit bureaus will not delete the account. Like the validation letter, the verbiage for a deletion letter is very specific (again, I will provide a template for you). It reports that the reason you are requesting the deletion is because the creditor could not validate the account at your request.

The creditor then must send proof that you signed for the account within thirty days. For this reason, all correspondence should be via certified mail.

If an account is verified as valid but the amount owed is more than you are able to pay, you may be able to negotiate a settlement for the debt. There are industry standards for an acceptable settlement range based on the length of time after your default date:

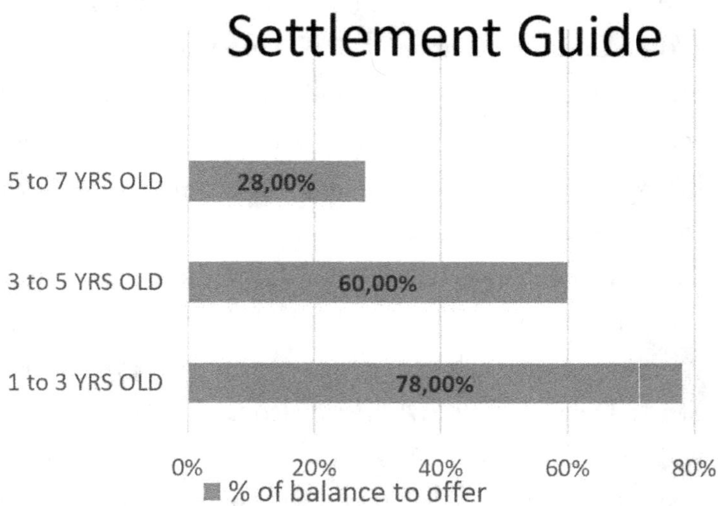

The left side of the settlement guide shows years after default date. The bottom of the guide shows the percentage of the balance left to offer.

For example, if an account is one to three years old, the acceptable percentage of the balance to settle the debt is 78. So, let's say you owe $3,760 on a two-year-old account. Your offer to the creditor should be 78 percent, or around $2,932.

The settlement guide is not an exact science. Of course, you can offer any amount to settle, even if it doesn't fit the chart. However, since compliance of the proposed settlement amount is solely up to the creditors, it makes sense to make an offer that has the greatest chance of being accepted. My advice is to offer the lowest amount of the category, understanding that you may have to pay more.

Now let's discuss charge-offs. A charge-off occurs when a creditor, after attempting to collect on a debt, deems the account uncollectible and writes it off as a loss for their own accounting purposes. As a result of the charge-off, the account is typically closed, and you can no longer use it.

This is important: Even though the account is charged off, you are still legally obligated to pay the debt. At the end of this book, you will find a charge-off template that can be used to acknowledge the debt, explain your reason for not being able to pay (e.g., job loss, death in the family), and offer to pay an amount in exchange for the company to report the account as "paid as agreed."

Changing the status of a charge-off is just as challenging as getting a company to settle for a lesser amount because it is at their discretion. The one advantage you have is the fact that currently they are getting no money toward the debt, and you are offering to pay a portion of it. The idea of getting any money may be attractive to them, since they'll want to minimize their own losses.

A creditor may sell your charged-off debt to a collection agency, who will then attempt to collect the outstanding balance. That's when you will see the status on your credit report change from the original creditor. Tip: A collection account is a good account to use when it comes to sending a validation letter.

Feel free to use the templates I'm providing at the end of this book in an email but be sure you get a response in writing that says the creditor agrees to your terms. If there is no response, use certified mail. (See Credit Repair Templates pgs. 130-138)

What If I Mess Up?

Messing up is inevitable, and I know all too well what that looks like. I married young, before I fully understood credit, and purchased a home with my husband in his name. On top of that, utility payments were not reported to credit agencies at that time. So, when we got divorced, I didn't really have any credit of my own.

I did, however, have a commercial cleaning business that had to be dissolved. Upon returning to Michigan, I was referred to a tax person who filed under my personal SSN instead of my business, making it look like I worked all year and never paid taxes. The problem didn't just go away like I wanted it to, and the tax penalties kept adding up as I tried to get help amending the returns.

Ultimately, I was able to get all the fees removed and was only obligated to pay the taxes owed—$4,000 instead of $22,000! (Bills don't disappear; they just multiply.) Once the bankruptcy was discharged, I applied for a credit card and bought a used car with a low loan balance. Paying both off quickly enabled me to build my own credit, despite my initially high interest rate.

All this to say, life happens. Job loss, change in marital status, death in the family, and so many other events can lead to you accumulating debt and your credit score taking a hit. But these things don't have to last.

Here are some steps to take to reestablish credit after experiencing a financial blow:

1. **Pay your bills on time:** This habit will eventually positively impact your score. It will also restore faith in lenders of your reliability in paying debts.
2. **Apply for a loan, using savings as collateral:** Much like using a paid-off vehicle as collateral, using your savings as collateral lets a lender know that you are willing to take a risk and not just asking them to take a risk by lending to you.
3. **Apply for a limited-use credit card:** Also known as a secured card, this type of card only allows you to use the amount that you have set aside. The purpose of a secured card is to again show lenders that you are putting up your own money in an effort to gain better financial status. If a company offers you a $300 secured card, you will provide them with $300 that they will hold in a separate account for a period until you have shown enough on-time payments. The length of time that the money must be held as security varies, but typically after twelve months of positive payments, the company will release and return the secured funds deposit to you.

4. **Apply for a loan with a cosigner:** This is a tricky one since the responsibility of the debt is shared with someone else. However, it is the quickest way to begin rebuilding your credit if someone more established is willing to sign on the dotted line with you on an account.
5. **Establish a steady work record:** The best way to prove you are a reliable person to lend to is by showing yourself responsible in work history. Lenders like to see a person who exhibits steady work history because it shows ability to pay.
6. **Open a checking account and don't overdraw it:** This action may seem like a no-brainer, but it must be said. Overdrawing an account doesn't look good when you need to supply bank statements for underwriter approval. Even worse is letting an account be overdrawn long enough for the bank to write your account off as a loss, which can end up on your credit report as a collection.
7. **Apply for a local store credit card and make regular monthly payments:** When reestablishing credit, it may be easier to get approved for credit cards from major retail stores. Doing so and making the payments on time will boost your credit score.

Remember, the #1 way to reestablish credit is to pay your bills on time. Doing so will improve your score organically over time.

There are plenty of credit repair companies and individuals who claim to magically fix your credit within a day, week, or month. *Do not give your money to them.* I'm here to tell you: There is nothing on your credit report that you cannot fix yourself. And if you have a couple thousand to spare, that money would be better spent paying off your balances.

A less than favorable financial picture did not happen overnight. Your credit score did not dip low over the weekend. So, what makes you think you can wave a wand and magically improve your financial circumstances?

Be patient and kind to yourself. You truly can make your financial dreams a reality by setting clear financial goals and creating a specific spending plan.

Something to Think About...

How many credit cards do you have? Why?

What are the balances and interest rates?

When are payments due?

When is the interest calculated?

What is your payment cycle? (beginning/end)

If you don't have credit cards:

- Research three credit card companies.
- Compare their interest rates and amenities.

Then write down which card you would choose and why:

Tell your younger self something about credit that you wish someone had told you:

Remember, you are entitled to a free credit report every twelve months from each of the major consumer reporting companies. You can request a copy from www.AnnualCreditReport.com one of three ways:

- Visit www.annualcreditreport.com
- Call 1-877-322-8228
- Write a letter to the Annual Credit Report Request Service: P.O. Box 105281, Atlanta, GA 30348-5281

CHAPTER 4

Setting Goals and Creating Plans

You may be thinking, *I've gone this far without having clear goals for my money—why should I have set goals now?* Well, financial goals help you determine where you are and where you want to be financially, as well as what you have to do to get there and how long will it take.

While creating a spending plan and analyzing it, you will discover that any goal costs money. For this reason, you must ask yourself if you are willing to do whatever it takes to meet your goals. Even if you learn from the numbers that you need to eliminate leisure activities to do so. The desire to be in a better position financially is just as important as being able to execute actionable steps toward your goals.

Setting financial goals requires you to rank your goals according to your values, priorities, dreams, and reality. We will spend more time defining these terms later on in this chapter, but for now, know that examining these things as a household is a crucial first step. Then you will need to define and prioritize your goals, create a plan, and put that plan into action.

I know you're excited about reaching new financial goals with the information you are learning, but let's first discuss some challenges on the road to improving your financial picture. The fact of the matter is, now all goals will be reached.

Here are some reasons why financial goals fail:

- **Unrealistic:** If you are trying to reach a savings goal of $500 per month, but your surplus monthly is $300, then your savings goal is not realistic and will need to be adjusted. In order for a plan to be realistic, it cannot be based on your dreams.
- **Lack of Discipline:** You must be willing to stick to the action steps you set in place to reach the goal. The most successful people are able to diligently stick to their spending plan.
- **Inconsistent Tracking Methods:** Many people are inconsistent with tracking expenses because they make purchases with cash. Once cash is gone, you forget where you spent it. Debit cards give you a clear picture of your spending.

If you experience any or a combination of these things, your spending plan is flawed and must be revisited immediately.

It's been said that people daydream multiple times a day, meaning that you typically spend more time thinking about doing things than actually doing them. So, let's start addressing the reasons why financial goals fail by looking at practical ways of making them more achievable.

How Do I Set Achievable Goals?

If your best friend said, "I want to save $10,000," you'd probably cheer them on. It's a clear enough goal, right? But without a process, that declaration is just a wish.

Similarly, it's human nature to want to live a long life, but many people fail to maintain a healthy lifestyle because they have a vague goal of exercising regularly. What if you set a goal of running a five-mile marathon this year? Could you do that successfully without first practicing one mile? You could try, but I'm willing to bet you would fall apart on the pavement before the finish line.

Think about goals as an event that requires well-thought-out and executed plans, not a single jump but a ladder with many steps. The first step? Identifying your values, priorities, dreams, and reality.

Values, Priorities, Dreams, and Reality

There are several factors that impact how you spend money, even if you haven't taken the time to examine your why. These factors are values, priorities, dreams, and reality:

- **Values** are the principles that govern your behavior, from everyday decisions to financial ones. For example, if you believe that stealing is wrong, no matter how much you want money, you will not go rob a bank to get it.
- **Priorities** are the things in your life that are the most important or urgent to you. If you have a child graduating high school and planning on receiving higher education, for instance,

saving toward their college fund may be at the top of your priority list.

- **Dreams** describe where you want to be and what you want to do, in this case financially. They're tricky because they can be realistic or unrealistic depending on your situation. All too often our imagination doesn't align with our reality.
- **Reality** showcases what you can actually do, such as how you will spend your income. Each idea before this was intangible, a theory, so to speak. But while you can dream of being debt-free next month, your income will determine what a realistic timeline is.

Vocalizing your spending motivators is an eye-opening experience. Take some time now to think about the things you value most.

Once you've identified your values, priorities, dreams, and reality, start generating potential short- and long-term goals. With the right planning, you *can* make your dreams a reality, but remember, not all goals are created equal. To ensure that your goals are achievable, make them SMART.

SMART Goals

SMART goals are specific, measurable, attainable, realistic, and time-bound. Knowing this, let's turn your friend's declaration of wanting to save $10,000 into a SMART goal:

- **Specific:** Your friend wants to save $10,000 in one year.
- **Measurable:** How much would they have to save each month?

  - $10,000 (total savings) / 12 (months) = $833 (monthly contribution)
- **Attainable:** Is $833/month feasible for your friend? What would they be willing to sacrifice to set aside that much money on a monthly basis?
- **Realistic:** Here's where expectation meets reality. Your friend would have to determine their monthly surplus—their net income (what they receive after taxes are deducted) minus their expenses.
  - $3,677.44 (monthly income) - $3,000 (expenses) = $677.44 (surplus)
  - Right now, your friend would not have enough surplus to save $833/month.
- **Time-Bound:** We determined one year is not a realistic timeframe for your friend to save $10,000, but they shouldn't just give up. They can instead determine a timeframe based on how much money they can comfortably put aside each month, like $500.
  - $10,000 (total savings) / $500 (monthly contribution) = 20 (months to reach goal)

You'll notice that the SMART method is great for managing expectations. Maybe your friend couldn't save $10,000 in one year, but they can in less than two!

Let's try another example, planning a family vacation:

- **Specific:** You want to go on vacation to Jamaica but don't know when.
- **Measurable:** You research the cost of the trip for a family of four.

  - Round-trip cost = $6,000
- **Attainable:** This isn't applicable yet because you must determine what your surplus is before you decide the amount of money you can feasibly set aside each month.
- **Realistic:** Remember, Net Income – Expenses = Surplus or Deficit.
  - $3,086 (monthly income) – $2,712 (expenses) = $374 (surplus)
  - With $374 in surplus, you decide that $200/month is an attainable amount to put toward the Jamaica vacation goal.
- **Time-Bound:** The time it takes to save $6,000 can be calculated by dividing the total cost by your monthly contribution.
  - $6,000 (total cost) / $200 (monthly contribution) = 30 months or 2½ years to save enough using your current income status

Once you've determined what's realistic and established a timeframe, you can go back to the top and make your goal more specific. Choose what month you want to vacation (e.g., July) and subtract thirty months to find out when you should start saving or making payments to a travel agent. Working the SMART method out of order is not ideal, but as you can see, it still works!

I want to note that the SMART method can be applied to any goal. For instance, if you want to start reading two books per month, you can figure out how many hours you need to read per day and break up that time into manageable chunks throughout each day. Or you can specify which books you want to read and calculate how many chapters you need to read each day.

You get the picture. The SMART method can and should be applied to any goal you want to achieve, especially the financial ones!

How Do I Create a Spending Plan?

When determining eligibility for loans, lenders look at your gross monthly income, but when creating a spending plan you can stick to, you need to look at your *net income*. This distinction is important because your gross monthly income is the amount before taxes, and your net income is what you actually bring home after taxes and deductions.

As you're creating your spending plan, don't forget to include all family members. This practice helps everyone in the household understand the family's financial goals and helps a child understand why they can't have McDonald's every week.

Net Income

To determine your gross monthly income, add up any money you receive from the following or any additional sources:

- Wages from work
- Commission
- Bonuses
- Child support
- Social Security
- Food Stamps

- Welfare payments
- Side jobs

Subtract your taxes and deductions to determine net income. This is the amount you will use to create your spending plan.

Let's say your gross income is $2,500 and your net income is $2,000. If your expenses are $1,800 and you create a spending plan based on your gross income, you might think you have $700 surplus each month. In actuality, you only have $200 surplus.

Remember, lenders determine eligibility based on gross income; they don't care if you can actually afford the monthly payment. So, according to them, you could take on a $250/month loan, but as a consumer, you should know your real surplus/deficit numbers. That way, you can say no to anything that will harm your budget and potentially your credit.

Note that while I think of the terms "spending plan" and "budget" interchangeably, I'm largely using the former because "budget" can put people on edge. People like to feel in control of their finances, not like someone else is telling them what to do, and "budget" sounds restrictive. "Spending plan," in contrast, speaks to how you can best make the money you have work for your current and future goals.

You should also consider wants versus needs when creating a spending plan. Wants and needs are unique to each person and are the innate drivers of our spending habits. No one plan will look like another for this reason.

Let's dive deeper into expenses so you can create a solid spending plan.

Expenses

To determine your monthly expenses, review your bank statements and/or online account activity for the past month. This will be more accurate than trying to remember how you spent the money. You should also list anything on your credit report (e.g., credit cards, auto/home/personal loans) and regular monthly expenses (e.g., rent, utilities, groceries, eating out, fuel, incidentals, personal care, tuition, entertainment).

Review this list of various expenses to ensure you're not leaving anything out:

- **Fixed expenses** are your payments that stay the same every month, such as rent, childcare, tuition, auto payments, insurance, mortgage, and student loans.
- **Flexible expenses** are those you have some control over, including food, utilities, and clothing.
- **Occasional expenses** come irregularly. They might include things like car insurance and gifts for holi-days and special occasions.
- **Indebted expenses** are the minimum monthly payments for your credit cards.
- **Intentional debt reduction** involves paying more than the minimum monthly payment on things like credit cards and other revolving debt.

Let's take a moment to look at the budget sheet provided on the next page. You can also use a different one from your online banking website or mobile app.

monthly budget

INCOME SOURCE	AMOUNT
TOTAL:	

NOTES

FIXED EXPENSES	BUDGET	SPENT
TOTAL:		

VARIABLE EXPENSES	BUDGET	SPENT
TOTAL:		

SAVING FOR?	SAVED
TOTAL SAVED:	

DEBT	PAID
TOTAL PAID:	

__________ - __________ = __________

TOTAL BUDGET TOTAL SPENT

Write the monies you received during the past month under the income source section, then write down what you spend under the fixed and variable expenses sections. (Using a statement from the past month will give you the most accurate financial picture, since that month is already completed.) Subtract your expenses from your net income to calculate your monthly surplus/deficit. If your calculation comes out negatively, that means your expenses exceed your income.

Next, write down the projected expenses for the current month under the budget column. Once you have paid those expenses, put the actual amount in the spent column. This will help you keep track of your budget in real time.

Americans primarily have direct deposit set up, and some keep enough money in their account that they don't see an extra $100 leave. People generally only notice overspending when their account is overdrawn, so if they keep positive funds in their account, they may never notice a deficit. In contrast, what I have noticed from working in banking is that account holders who don't have excess funds tend to check their accounts more often and are more likely to notice ahead of time when a bill may not clear.

Remember, the purpose of keeping track of your daily transactions is to catch potential financial issues before they negatively impact you.

My Budget Shows a Surplus?

If your spending plan shows a surplus, that means you have the opportunity to save for kids' activities, emergencies, insurance payments, a down payment, or something as simple as gift giving. Take a moment to think about what you could do with surplus money—specifically, how you can make the money work for your future. I know it is tempting to think of spending money on fun experiences, but I challenge you to first revisit your goals.

As I've said, debt is the killer of wealth building. The more debt you have, and the longer you hold on to it, the further you are away from reaching your ultimate wealth goals. So, before you plan for a big vacation, let me share some tips for reducing your debt.

Intentional Debt Reduction

The more liabilities you have, the less net worth you have. It's a simple formula: **Assets – Liabilities = Net Worth**.

You may remember that we briefly discussed intentional debt reduction earlier in this chapter. Two common ways to intentionally reduce using your surplus are the snowball and avalanche methods:

Snowball	Paying off debts from lowest balance to highest balance
Avalanche	Paying off debts from highest interest rate to lowest interest rate

I recommend the snowball method for clients who need to see milestone wins as motivation to keep going. For them, rapid results fuel their drive to complete the next goal.

Other clients insist on using the avalanche method, paying the minimum required payment on all debt plus whatever amount they have set aside for the loan with the highest interest rate. This might just be an extra $10 per month. Another avalanche strategy is paying off the debt that is affecting your DTI ratio the most so you can get your percentage below 30.

Note: The right method for you may not be what you think. I encourage you to discuss options with a competent financial advisor.

If you have a surplus each month and no debt, consider, do you have an emergency fund? An emergency fund is an account that includes enough money to cover three to six months' worth of your expenses. (Your budget really comes in handy for knowing what balance should be in your emergency fund.) Another goal you might consider is saving for a down payment on a home or purchasing a used vehicle.

Whatever your financial goals are, having a clear spending plan allows you to see what you are spending monthly and if you can stash away for bigger purchases. It also allows you to create savings.

Savings

Let's face it, saving money is not the most fun activity in the world, but there are a few ways you can choose to build your savings. One way is the "pay yourself first" method. Some people really love this method because it gives them joy to know they are putting money toward their own goals before doing anything else with their paycheck.

The next way to mindlessly save money is to sign up for any "keep the change" programs with your bank or credit card. These programs automatically deposit the difference between what you spent on a purchase and the next dollar amount into a savings account of your choosing. For example, if you purchase $75.65 worth of goods, a "keep the change" program with that card will deposit 35 cents into your savings.

Another way to save is to deposit any unexpected money, such as inheritance checks or tax returns, into a savings account. These types of windfalls can catapult your savings.

If you're a spender, you can open a savings account that is not easy to access in person and opt out of an ATM card. The point of saving toward a goal is to make sure your money is working the way you intend it to, so this ensures you aren't tempted to withdraw funds unnecessarily. After all, if you don't give your money a place to go, it will go wherever it wants quickly.

In recent years, the 100-envelope challenge has become a popular way to save. (I believe the popularity increased because the use of the envelope makes it feel like a fun game, especially when using decorative or monogramed plastic envelopes.) The concept is simple: You number envelopes 1 to 100 and start putting the amount specified inside each (i.e., $57 in Envelope #57). Some people stretch this challenge out over the course of a year, and some do it multiple times each year. Either way, if you complete the challenge, you'll save $5,050.

Other people like the fifty-two-week savings because it requires less investment, but some find it difficult because it requires weekly savings. This challenge asks that you save $1 per week. Which doesn't seem like a lot…at first. The difficulty comes once the weeks progress and require $30, then $31, and even on to $50 per week. Having a weekly surplus available to save is a challenge for most, making this unrealistic for the majority. However, if you can make it to the end of this challenge, you will save $1,378. (See Diagram)

52 WEEK MONEY CHALLENGE

Week	Deposit Amount	Account Balance		Week	Deposit Amount	Account Balance
1	$1.00	$1.00		27	$27.00	$378.00
2	$2.00	$3.00		28	$28.00	$406.00
3	$3.00	$6.00		29	$29.00	$435.00
4	$4.00	$10.00		30	$30.00	$465.00
5	$5.00	$15.00		31	$31.00	$496.00
6	$6.00	$21.00		32	$32.00	$528.00
7	$7.00	$28.00		33	$33.00	$561.00
8	$8.00	$36.00		34	$34.00	$595.00
9	$9.00	$45.00		35	$35.00	$630.00
10	$10.00	$55.00		36	$36.00	$666.00
11	$11.00	$66.00		37	$37.00	$703.00
12	$12.00	$78.00		38	$38.00	$741.00
13	$13.00	$91.00		39	$39.00	$780.00
14	$14.00	$105.00		40	$40.00	$820.00
15	$15.00	$120.00		41	$41.00	$861.00
16	$16.00	$136.00		42	$42.00	$903.00
17	$17.00	$153.00		43	$43.00	$946.00
18	$18.00	$171.00		44	$44.00	$990.00
19	$19.00	$190.00		45	$45.00	$1,035.00
20	$20.00	$210.00		46	$46.00	$1,081.00
21	$21.00	$231.00		47	$47.00	$1,128.00
22	$22.00	$253.00		48	$48.00	$1,176.00
23	$23.00	$276.00		49	$49.00	$1,125.00
24	$24.00	$300.00		50	$50.00	$1,275.00
25	$25.00	$325.00		51	$51.00	$1,326.00
26	$26.00	$351.00		52	$52.00	$1,378.00

A predominant amount of people are paid biweekly, and according to the Bank of America Institute (October 2024), approximately 30 percent of the population are living paycheck to paycheck. Because of this fact, it makes sense that a biweekly savings plan would be more feasible for most people.

Take a look at a couple biweekly savings plans:

- $10 per pay period: $10 x 26 weeks = $260/year
- $30 per pay period: $30 x 26 weeks = $780/year

You can always increase the minimum amount to save; just keep it at a comfortable number that won't be missed. If you keep having to take from it, then it's not savings, and you'll need to readjust your plan. You won't miss $10 per pay period, but your savings account will notice the growth if you can stick with it.

Now, I know I just stated that it's hard for most people to save weekly—biweekly is more realistic—but I'm going to introduce you to a daily savings challenge: the 365-day money challenge. The difference between the weekly challenge and this one is the amounts: one penny on the first day, two on the second day, and so on. (See Diagram)

PENNY SAVINGS *Challenge*

0.01	0.32	0.63	0.94	1.25	1.56	1.87	2.18	2.49	2.80	3.11	3.42
0.02	0.33	0.64	0.95	1.26	1.57	1.88	2.19	2.50	2.81	3.12	3.43
0.03	0.34	0.65	0.96	1.27	1.58	1.89	2.20	2.51	2.82	3.13	3.44
0.04	0.35	0.66	0.97	1.28	1.59	1.90	2.21	2.52	2.83	3.14	3.45
0.05	0.36	0.67	0.98	1.29	1.60	1.91	2.22	2.53	2.84	3.15	3.46
0.06	0.37	0.68	0.99	1.30	1.61	1.92	2.23	2.54	2.85	3.16	3.47
0.07	0.38	0.69	1.00	1.31	1.62	1.93	2.24	2.55	2.86	3.17	3.48
0.08	0.39	0.70	1.01	1.32	1.63	1.94	2.25	2.56	2.87	3.18	3.49
0.09	0.40	0.71	1.02	1.33	1.64	1.95	2.26	2.57	2.88	3.19	3.50
0.10	0.41	0.72	1.03	1.34	1.65	1.96	2.27	2.58	2.89	3.20	3.51
0.11	0.42	0.73	1.04	1.35	1.66	1.97	2.28	2.59	2.90	3.21	3.52
0.12	0.43	0.74	1.05	1.36	1.67	1.98	2.29	2.60	2.91	3.22	3.53
0.13	0.44	0.75	1.06	1.37	1.68	1.99	2.30	2.61	2.92	3.23	3.54
0.14	0.45	0.76	1.07	1.38	1.69	2.00	2.31	2.62	2.93	3.24	3.55
0.15	0.46	0.77	1.08	1.39	1.70	2.01	2.32	2.63	2.94	3.25	3.56
0.16	0.47	0.78	1.09	1.40	1.71	2.02	2.33	2.64	2.95	3.26	3.57
0.17	0.48	0.79	1.10	1.41	1.72	2.03	2.34	2.65	2.96	3.27	3.58
0.18	0.49	0.80	1.11	1.42	1.73	2.04	2.35	2.66	2.97	3.28	3.59
0.19	0.50	0.81	1.12	1.43	1.74	2.05	2.36	2.67	2.98	3.29	3.60
0.20	0.51	0.82	1.13	1.44	1.75	2.06	2.37	2.68	2.99	3.30	3.61
0.21	0.52	0.83	1.14	1.45	1.76	2.07	2.38	2.69	3.00	3.31	3.62
0.22	0.53	0.84	1.15	1.46	1.77	2.08	2.39	2.70	3.01	3.32	3.63
0.23	0.54	0.85	1.16	1.47	1.78	2.09	2.40	2.71	3.02	3.33	3.64
0.24	0.55	0.86	1.17	1.48	1.79	2.10	2.41	2.72	3.03	3.34	3.65
0.25	0.56	0.87	1.18	1.49	1.80	2.11	2.42	2.73	3.04	3.35	
0.26	0.57	0.88	1.19	1.50	1.81	2.12	2.43	2.74	3.05	3.36	
0.27	0.58	0.89	1.20	1.51	1.82	2.13	2.44	2.75	3.06	3.37	
0.28	0.59	0.90	1.21	1.52	1.83	2.14	2.45	2.76	3.07	3.38	
0.29	0.60	0.91	1.22	1.53	1.84	2.15	2.46	2.77	3.08	3.39	
0.30	0.61	0.92	1.23	1.54	1.85	2.16	2.47	2.78	3.09	3.40	
0.31	0.62	0.93	1.24	1.55	1.86	2.17	2.48	2.79	3.10	3.41	

$667.95 Saved

Even in this economy, just about everyone can afford to save a couple pennies each day. Plus, you quickly become used to setting aside money, since it only takes thirteen days to create a habit. At the end of this challenge, you will save $667.95.

If you're someone who saves regularly but isn't putting the money in one place, label your savings accounts based on your goals. How many accounts you have will depend on your lifestyle and your ability to manage multiple accounts.

Below are several savings accounts you might have:

- Lump sum (for paying off monthly expenses)
- General savings (unexpected expenses)
- Emergency fund (large, unexpected costs)
- Sinking fund (large future expense)
- Repair reserve account (home)
- Repair reserve account (car)
- Car replacement fund
- Sinking fund – travel
- Sinking fund – home décor
- Sinking fund – gifts
- Certificate of Deposit (CD)

I know what you're thinking…that's an excessive number of accounts to maintain. I agree, but it works for some people for two reasons. First, it means the household has the same savings goals. Second, everyone involved understands how to use their savings.

You may not need a fund set aside for home décor or gifts, but you may have a side hustle or second job that you took in an effort to reach a particular goal, like going on a vacation. In that case, you may decide to create an account that only holds money from that income so you can better track the balance toward that goal.

There is no standard for number of accounts. You can have as many or few as you want as long as you are using a system you and your household understand.

Whatever you decide to try to start saving, just do it. You'll thank yourself later.

What If I Show a Monthly Deficit?

Once you've created a spending plan, check it often to ensure you are staying on target. Ask yourself, *Am I reaching my short-term goals? Am I facing any challenges in reaching those goals?* Challenges might range from inflation to pay cuts.

Let's say you originally planned on spending $300 per month on groceries, but you have exceeded that amount for more than two months. That's a sign your spending plan needs to be revisited. Anytime you are consistently not matching the projected spending for a category, you should review your plan. That way, you can adjust quickly, before the discrepancies have a negative impact on your financial picture.

Another way to see if you are overspending in a category is to use the Spending Plan Pie Chart, which shows how much of your monthly income should be allocated toward certain expenses. (See Diagram)

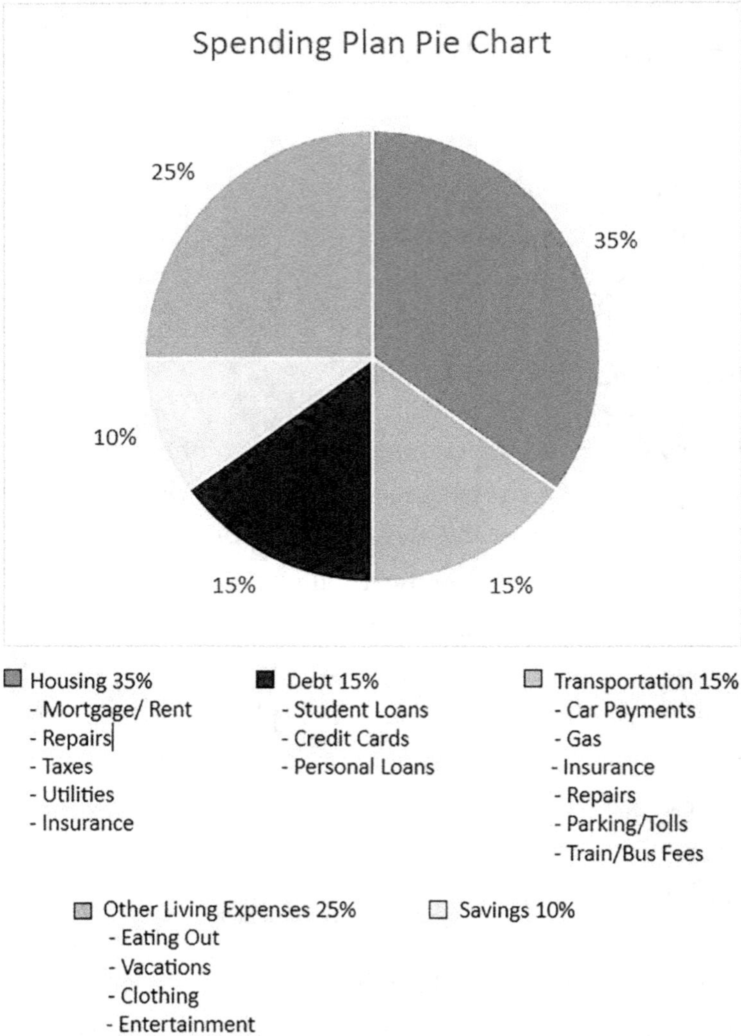

According to researchers, for optimal financial success, no more than 35 percent of your income should go toward housing, 25 percent toward other living expenses, 15 percent toward debt (items on your credit report), and 15 percent toward transportation needs. That way, 10 percent can go toward savings.

If you are showing a negative monthly amount, you'll need to examine options to impact your money. The options are to increase your income to match your current expenses or to spend less. In severe cases, you may need to do both simultaneously.

I often ask clients to examine their nonessential self-care habits, like getting massages, visiting the nail salon, or going on trips. I also ask them about in-home luxuries, such as cable and subscriptions. These things are fun but not necessary when a goal is in reach. I encourage my clients to instead focus on their four walls—anything that directly impacts how their household runs daily, including housing payments, utility bills, transportation expenses, and debt payments. No eating out, movies, or expensive outings.

Most are not willing to make these sacrifices. Society has us believing that doing more is what's best, but doing more when you don't have more kills your financial success.

After reviewing your spending plan, you may determine that you're already operating at the lowest expense you can while maintaining your household. Or you may determine that decreasing expenses is not something you are willing to do at this time. In those cases, you'll need to increase your income. If a traditional second job doesn't fit your schedule, you might look at work-from-home jobs or delivery driver options like DoorDash, Uber Eats, and Instacart.

If, after decreasing expenses and increasing income, you're still struggling to make ends meet, you'll need to restructure your spending plan and adjust your SMART goals accordingly. Typically, either increasing income or decreasing expenses alone will work to bring an individual to the surplus side of their budget. However, reviewing your plan regularly will keep you on track.

Reviewing your plan consists of asking yourself, *What costs are consistently off?* The easiest way to get this answer is to refer back to your budget, which shows the projected amount versus what you actually spent. For example, are you overpaying for internet service or energy? Everything should be assessed for efficiency, then adjusted accordingly. Expense categories with discrepancies will be the ones to address first.

The point is, you can get creative with how you're setting and achieving your financial goals, no matter your budget. Plus, learning to do so will help you throughout life, including as you're planning for retirement.

Something to Think About...

If you are paid every other week, then two months each year you will receive three paychecks. Many people use these "extra" pay periods to pay down their debt, contribute more to savings, or make a special purchase that they normally wouldn't be able to afford. Others use them to catch up because they are living beyond their means.

Which type of bill paying would you rather do—"paying down" or "catching up"? Why?

Write at least three things you can do to improve your current financial situation:

Which saving strategy appeals to you most? Why?

List your financial goals.

Make them SMART goals.

CHAPTER 5

Looking Toward Retirement

Planning for retirement was not at the forefront of my mind in college and in my twenties. Even working in the banking industry did not make me more interested in the topic. No one really wants to think about winding down; retirement planning can feel almost like planning your own burial service.

Because I had little understanding of retirement accounts as a young adult, every time I switched jobs, I would take everything out of my 401(k) and accept the penalty. I didn't know you could set up a retirement account that was separate from your employer, so I started from zero at each company instead of building on my existing balance. I wasn't worried because I thought I'd have plenty of time to save.

Later on, I left a job and lost everything I'd put in for three years, plus their matched amount. I didn't understand that their vesting period meant I would have to work there for five years for them to feel like they got their money's worth—and for me to get my investment back. I didn't understand that vesting periods are put in place to deter employee turnover, since statistics show most people stay with a company once they reach the five-year mark. Not understanding these things ultimately cost me thousands of dollars.

As they say, the best time to start retirement planning was yesterday; the next best time is today. So, let me tell you everything I've learned about 401(k)s, IRAs, life insurance, and more so that you don't make the same mistakes I did.

But Won't I Have Time to Save?

As soon as you are gainfully employed, you should begin saving for retirement, but we often put off doing so. Listen closely: *There is no such thing as making up for lost time.*

First, decide when you want to retire and find out how much money you'll need to maintain your lifestyle. Second, using the SMART method, calculate how much you'll need to save monthly to make this goal achievable. Remember that while people tend to have fewer needs and wants as they get older, prices continue to rise, making everyday living more expensive.

Planning for retirement looks different for everyone, and no one plan is correct. This is due to our differing value systems. What you feel is necessary for your comfort during retirement will differ from friends, even from a spouse. For this reason, couples should consider what retirement will look like for their household together.

It is also important to work with people who have expertise in areas that you are not well-versed in. For example, I reached out to a financial advisor who could help me invest my money for maximum growth.

To maintain your finances after you leave the workforce, you need to create a detailed retirement plan. We'll discuss what that involves next.

Steps for Retirement Planning

You may be wondering, *How do I begin retirement planning?* There are five basic steps:

1. **Know when to start retirement planning:** The earlier you start planning, the more time your money has to grow.
2. **Figure out how much money you need to retire:** The typical advice is to replace 70 to 90 percent of your annual pre-retirement income through savings and Social Security.
3. **Prioritize your financial goals:** Retirement is probably not your only savings goal. Other financial goals include paying down credit card or student loan debt and building up an emergency fund.
4. **Select your retirement investments:** Determining the right mix of investments depends on how long you have until you need the money and how comfortable you are with risk.
5. **Choose the best retirement plan for you:** The cornerstone of retirement planning is determining not only how much to save but also where to save it. The best plans provide tax advantages and, if available, additional savings incentives like matching contributions.

The earliest you can start claiming Social Security benefits is age 62. However, if you file early, you'll sacrifice a portion of your benefits.

Scan the code to check your claiming age. (Planning Social Security Claiming Age, CFPB)

Common Types of Retirement Plans

There are so many types of retirement plans that it can be confusing and discouraging trying to pick. In this section, I will share the main differences so you can make informed decisions.

A **401(k)** is a retirement savings and investing plan that employers offer. Depending on the type of plan you have, the tax break comes either when you contribute money or when you withdraw it during retirement. Many employers offer to match a portion of what you save; this is the perk that gets all the headlines.

Quick 401(k) facts:

- Elective salary deferrals are excluded from the employee's taxable income
- Employers can contribute to employees' accounts.

- Distributions, including earnings, are includible in taxable income at retirement

A **traditional IRA** is a way to save for retirement that gives you tax advantages. For example, if your income is $60,000 and you contribute $6,000 to a traditional IRA, then your taxable income that year will drop to $54,000.

Quick traditional IRA facts:

- There are typically contribution limits.
- Contributions you make to a traditional IRA may be fully or partially tax deductible, depending on your filing status and income.
- Generally, amounts in your traditional IRA (including earnings and gains) are not taxed until you take a distribution (withdrawal) from your IRA.

Roth IRAs give you tax-free withdrawals after retirement, where traditional IRAs give you a tax break beforehand. If you like the idea of tax-free income in retirement, Roth IRAs are a good idea.

Quick Roth IRA facts:

- The account or annuity must be designated as a Roth IRA when it is set up.
- If, at age 59½, you've held the account for at least five years, distributions and earnings can be withdrawn without paying federal taxes.
- Qualified distributions of investment earnings are tax-free but unadvisable.

- You can withdraw your original contribution at any time without penalty.
- You can contribute to your Roth IRA after you reach age 70½, as well as leave amounts in your Roth IRA as long as you live.

SEP IRAs (Simplified Employee Pensions) are for business owners. Investments grow tax-deferred until retirement, when distributions are taxed as income, and then they are tax deductible.

Quick SEP IRA facts:

- It is available to any size business.
- It is easily established by adopting Form 5305-SEP PDF. There's no filing requirement for the employer.
- Only the employer contributes to traditional SEP-IRAs set up for each eligible employee.
- Employees are always 100 percent vested in (or have ownership of) all SEP-IRA money.
- It can be combined with a traditional IRA or a Roth IRA.
- Contributions are tax-deductible, including those made to employee accounts.

A **SIMPLE IRA (Savings Incentive Match PLan for Employees)** allows employees and employers to contribute to traditional IRAs set up for employees. This is ideally suited as a start-up retirement savings plan for small employers not currently sponsoring a retirement plan.

This is because eligible employees invest a portion of their pretax salary into an individual account and receive mandatory employer contributions.

Quick SIMPLE IRA facts:

- Employer contributions vest immediately. You have 100 percent ownership of all the money in your SIMPLE IRA.
- Employees may elect to contribute.
- Each year, the employer must make a matching contribution up to 3 percent of each employee's pay or a nonelective contribution of 2 percent each eligible employee's pay.

A **SIMPLE 401(k)**, like the SIMPLE IRA, is a plan for small businesses with 100 or fewer employees.

Quick SIMPLE 401(k) facts:

- An employee can elect to defer some compensation.
- Unlike a regular 401(k) plan, the employer must make a matching contribution up to 3 percent of each employee's pay or a nonelective contribution of 2 percent of each eligible employee's pay.

A **Solo 401(k)** isn't a new type of 401(k). It's a traditional 401(k) plan covering a business owner with no employees or that person and his or her spouse. The business owner wears two hats in a 401(k) plan: employee and employer.

Quick Solo 401(k) facts:

- The owner can contribute elective deferrals up to 100 percent of compensation ("earned income" in the case of a self-employed individual) up to the annual contribution limit.
- They can also make employer nonelective contributions up to 25 percent of compensation, as defined by the plan, or for self-employed individuals.

Not only do you need to choose a plan for retirement, but you also need to choose a life insurance policy that fits your needs. Having a basic understanding of how this type of insurance works will prevent you from being underinsured, so I will explain your options next.

Life Insurance

There are three main types of permanent life insurance: whole, universal, and variable. Keep in mind that the cost and availability of insurance depends on factors such as age, health, and the type and amount of insurance purchased.

Before choosing life insurance, it is prudent to make sure that you are insurable. Let's examine the main characteristics of each type.

Whole life insurance is a permanent life insurance with a premium that stays the same throughout the life of the policy.

Quick whole life insurance facts:

- Premiums can accumulate cash value and are invested in the company's general investment portfolio.
- You may be able to borrow funds from the cash value or surrender your policy for its face value, if necessary.

Universal life coverage has the same type of coverage and cash value as whole life but with greater flexibility.

Quick universal life coverage facts:

- Once money has accumulated in your cash-value account, you may be able to vary the frequency, as well as the amount, of your premiums.

- Altering your premiums may decrease the value of the death benefit.

With **variable life insurance**, you receive the same death protection as with other types of permanent life insurance, but you are given control over how your cash value is invested.

Quick variable life insurance facts:

- You have the option of investing your cash value in stocks, bonds, or money market funds.
- The value of your policy has the potential to grow more quickly, but there is also more risk.
- If your investments do not perform well, your cash value and the death benefit may decrease. However, some policies provide a guarantee that your death benefit will not fall below a certain level.
- Premiums for this type of insurance are fixed.

As with choosing a retirement plan, I recommend working with a licensed and experienced insurance agent. This can make all the difference in your planning process and ensure you are using your money wisely.

Where Do I Go from Here?

Retirement planning can feel overwhelming, so I'd like to leave you with a couple of nuggets.

First, your retirement plan won't look like anyone else's, so give yourself some grace if you don't have it all figured out on Day 1. If you need help planning, reach out to a trusted retirement advisor.

Second, you will experience a mental and financial adjustment when you leave the workforce. Prepare by implementing hobbies into your daily routine now. Plan visits with family that you don't often get to see. Make sure you're filling the void with activities that are meaningful to you.

You worked hard for retirement. With a solid plan in place, you can really enjoy it.

Something to Think About...

What are my retirement goals?

How much money will I need for living expenses?

Do I have a plan for long-term care?

Have I updated my estate plan?

Am I emotionally ready for retirement?

Do I need professional advice?

Final Words

My knowledge of managing finances doesn't just come from studying. It's a compilation of over 25 years within the financial industry, coupled with my lived experiences, and those of the various customers and clients I've helped. For example, as a young adult, my debit card was used by an unauthorized user, causing my account to be overdrawn. At the time, I kept my card and a written copy of my PIN on the desk in my bedroom because no one told me to keep them separate. I thought keeping them together would help me keep track!

My bedroom was connected to the main bathroom in the apartment, so I can only ascertain that my card was taken during an event with some college buddies. Of course, the bank didn't want to hear that because the point of having a PIN is that no one else knows it. My actions were just as foolish as choosing your birthday for your PIN. I was only saved from serious legal trouble because the camera at the ATM showed the face of a male using the card, and I was still responsible for the overdrawn money.

Trust me when I say, this experience deepened my hunger for financial knowledge. I kept thinking that if someone had shared the tiny tidbits with me, I could've avoided the situation altogether.

The do's, don'ts and loopholes shared here are not theories…they are industry facts.

Now that you've made it to the end of this book, you may be feeling overwhelmed with financial knowledge. I implore you not to run away from it but instead allow that feeling to be the catalyst for making drastic changes. I hope you take your financial power back using the tips I shared throughout this book.

As a reminder, we began this journey by discussing how our perception of and experiences with money influence our spending characteristics, but we can take ownership of our financial decisions. We then learned how financial institutions operate and how we can identify the right place to put our money based on our current financial needs.

Later, we talked about how you can't ignore debt, how the credit pie is the key to your success, and how SMART goal setting can turn wishes into actionable plans. More specifically, we determined our net income, expenses, and surplus/deficit and made a spending plan accordingly. Finally, we looked toward retirement, identifying what we'd need versus want and how we could start saving to get there.

My hope is that this book has given you the confidence to achieve your own definition of financial success, but please know that you are not alone on your financial journey. If you need additional assistance, my company, DG Revenue Management, offers individual counseling and coaching sessions. Either way, I'm cheering you on.

Always remember, there's growth on the other side of discomfort. Now go make your financial dreams a reality!

CREDIT REPAIR TEMPLATES

Account Validation Template

(Date)

To whom it may concern:

My name is **(Full Name)**. I am writing you in regard to an account that appears on my credit report **account number XXXXXXXXXXX**. At this time I am asking you to validate this debt. Under the law, I am entitled to a written response from your company. If you do not respond within 30 days, I will report to the three credit reporting agencies and ask it to be removed.

Once I receive validation on this debt from your company I will speak with them about further options. Please note that this letter is NOT an acknowledgment of this debt. Your validation response should include the following:

1. The name, number, and address of the original creditor as well as statements from the previous 12 months of this account.
2. I am requesting a signed copy of the original agreement for my records.
3. Proof that your company is authorized to collect this debt on behalf of the creditor.
4. The original date of delinquency with the debt.

Once again, if your company does not respond within 30 days this will be construed as a waiver of your claims against me. I am requesting that your company provide evidence and documentation that I have a legal obligation to you. Once again, this is not an acknowledgment of this debt. I am requesting this validation in writing and I do not want phone calls from your company.

Sincerely,

____

(First Name and Last Name)

Deletion Letter Template

(Date)

RE: DELETIONS TO CREDIT REPORT

To whom it may concern:
I received a copy of my credit report and am disputing some items that need to be deleted. I have highlighted and numbered these disputed items on the attached copy of my credit report. The reasons why these items should be deleted are indicated below:

Item #	Reason for Deletion
Account Name	Company unable to validate the account within 30 days from request.

Account Number: XXXXXXXXXXX

According to the provisions of the Fair Credit Reporting Act € 611(a) [15 USC 1681i(a)], these disputed items must be reinvestigated or deleted from my credit report within 30 days. In the interim, these items should be noted on my credit record as "in dispute." I am also requesting the names, addresses and telephone numbers of individuals you contacted during your investigation so that I may follow up.

Thank you,

____

(First Name and Last Name)

Settlement Letter Template

(Your Name)
(Your Street Address)
(Your City, State, Zip Code)

Complaint Department
(Company Name)
(Company Street Address)
(Company City, State, Zip Code)

Dear Creditor:

I am writing to you because I am finally in the position where I can offer a settlement offer.

You stated in your reporting to my credit report that I owe $______________. I am proposing a payment of $__________________ to settle this debt. I am currently in negotiations with other agencies and will only pay those that work with me and help me reach agreed-upon terms. This debt is from (month and year of the debt) and is near the statute of limitations. I personally feel an offer of (insert % offering) is quite reasonable.

In addition, I am requesting that your company report my account as PAID IN FULL once you have received payment. I am requesting a written response from your agency. If you agree to my terms, please state this in writing. I am again offering $proposed amount to settle this debt and I am asking that the debt be reported to all three credit reporting agencies as paid in full. Once you send me a letter stating you agree to these terms, I will immediately send you a cashier's check for $proposed amount. At that point I am requesting a statement from you showing that I have zero balance.

Again, I request that all communication be in writing. I will not make payment until I have in writing our agreed-upon terms.

Sincerely,

____

(First Name and Last Name)

Charge-Off Removal Template

(Date)

(Original Creditor/Name of Collection Agency, if the Account Was Sold)

(Creditor Address]

RE: [account ex: Citibank Mastercard] account # [full account number] *(if contacting a collection agency include the original account number, i.e., the Mastercard number in this case, and also include any account number assigned by the collection agency –this number would be on one of your collection letters)*

Dear Sir or Madam,

After recently reviewing my credit report, I took notice that the above-mentioned account is currently in [status of account, ex: Charge-Off] status. I sincerely would like to take care of this account as soon as possible.

Due to [whatever caused you to be late on your payments, ex: illness], I unfortunately got behind on my payments and was unable to meet my obligations. However, since then my situation has greatly improved and I am in the position to recompense this debt.

I am willing to pay [creditor's name] [x payments a month] equaling the amount of [total they are requesting] provided that the above account is updated on all credit reporting agencies to state: PAID AS AGREED, or completely removed from all credit reporting agencies upon my final payment.

I am not agreeing to an updated credit report that states this account as: "PAID CHARGE-OFF" or the like, as this will not significantly increase my credit score, nor will it reflect my sincere willingness to restore my good name and hopefully, someday, again do business with your company.

Your written response will serve as an agreement to my proposal and I will begin payments. Thank you very much for your valued time.

Best regards,

____

(First Name and Last Name)

(Your Street Address, City, State, Zip Code)

MONEY MANAGEMENT TOOLS

DEBT REDUCTION TRACKER

DEBT:		
BALANCE:		
MIN. PAYMENT:		
DATE	PAYMENT	BALANCE

DEBT:		
BALANCE:		
MIN. PAYMENT:		
DATE	PAYMENT	BALANCE

DEBT REDUCTION TRACKER

DEBT:		
BALANCE:		
MIN. PAYMENT:		
DATE	PAYMENT	BALANCE

DEBT:		
BALANCE:		
MIN. PAYMENT:		
DATE	PAYMENT	BALANCE

EXPENSES TRACKER

FIXED EXPENSES	AMOUNT
RENT/MORTGAGE	
ELECTRICITY	
WATER	
GAS	
INTERNET	
PHONE	

FOOD	AMOUNT
GROCERIES	
COFFEE	
SNACKS	

TRANSPORTATION	AMOUNT
FUEL	
MAINTENANCE	
PARKING FEES	
INSURANCE	
PUBLIC TRANSPORT	

ENTERTAINMENT	AMOUNT
MOVIES	
CONCERTS/EVENTS	
HOBBIES	
RESTAURANTS	
PARTIES	
LEISURE TRAVEL	

SHOPPING	AMOUNT
CLOTHES	
ELECTRONICS	
BEAUTY	
HOME GOODS	
GIFTS	

MEDICAL	AMOUNT
DOCTOR VISITS	
MEDICATIONS	
HEALTH INSURANCE	

FITNESS	AMOUNT
GYM MEMBERSHIPS	
SPORTS	
EQUIPMENT	
WELLNESS	
PRODUCTS	

FAMILY & EDUCATION	AMOUNT
CHILDCARE	
TUITION FEES	
BOOKS	
MATERIALS	
COURSES	

SUMMARY	

SPENDING PLANNER

INCOME	AMOUNT

BILLS	AMOUNT

SAVINGS	AMOUNT

EXPENSES	AMOUNT

DEBT	AMOUNT

SUMMARY	AMOUNT
INCOME	
BILLS	
SAVINGS	
EXPENSES	
DEBT	

SPENDING PLANNER

INCOME	AMOUNT

BILLS	AMOUNT

SAVINGS	AMOUNT

EXPENSES	AMOUNT

DEBT	AMOUNT

SUMMARY	AMOUNT
INCOME	
BILLS	
SAVINGS	
EXPENSES	
DEBT	

SIMPLE BUDGET TRACKER

NR	DATE	INCOME	DESCRIPTION	AMOUNT

NR	DATE	EXPENSE	DESCRIPTION	AMOUNT

SUMMARY	

SIMPLE BUDGET TRACKER

NR	DATE	INCOME	DESCRIPTION	AMOUNT

NR	DATE	EXPENSE	DESCRIPTION	AMOUNT

SUMMARY	

SAVINGS CHALLENGE

SAVING FOR:	GOAL:

MONTH	DATE	DEPOSIT	BALANCE	NOTES
January				
February				
March				
April				
May				
June				
July				
August				
September				
October				
November				
December				

SAVING FOR:	GOAL:

MONTH	DATE	DEPOSIT	BALANCE	NOTES
January				
February				
March				
April				
May				
June				
July				
August				
September				
October				
November				
December				

SAVINGS CHALLENGE

SAVING FOR:	GOAL:

MONTH	DATE	DEPOSIT	BALANCE	NOTES
January				
February				
March				
April				
May				
June				
July				
August				
September				
October				
November				
December				

SAVING FOR:	GOAL:

MONTH	DATE	DEPOSIT	BALANCE	NOTES
January				
February				
March				
April				
May				
June				
July				
August				
September				
October				
November				
December				

Downloadable
Financial Guides & Worksheets

Notes

Hanson, Melanie. "Average Student Loan Debt for a Bachelor's Degree" EducationData.org, October 13, 2024,

https://educationdata.org/average-debt-for-a-bachelors-degree

Rector, Connor - Senior Content Lead at Mitek. "42 check fraud statistics your bank can't ignore" 2025,

https://www.miteksystems.com/blog/42-check-fraud-statistics-your-bank-cant-ignore

https://www.creditrevitalize.com/

https://institute.bankofamerica.com/content/dam/economic-insights/paycheck-to-paycheck-lower-income-households.pdf,

(October 2024)

Connect with NaToya Jones, Financial Liaison

Thank you for trusting me to be part of your financial journey while taking the time to invest in your financial future. If you have questions, feedback, or want to continue your journey, I'd love to hear from you.

Email: info@dgrevmgmt.com
For reader feedback, speaking inquiries or collaboration opportunities.
www.dgrevmgmt.com\ Explore additional tools & resources.

Instagram: @dgrevenuemgmt

This book is intended to spark the conversation surrounding your financial well-being. For personalized guidance, please book a coaching session.

www.ingramcontent.com/pod-product-compliance
Lightning Source LLC
LaVergne TN
LVHW022057200926
848481LV00003B/950